WHAT
You Don't
KNOW
May Be
Killing You!

Don Colbert, M.D.

SILOAM
A Strang Company

WHAT YOU DON'T KNOW MAY BE KILLING YOU by Don Colbert, M.D.
Published by Siloam
A Strang Company
600 Rinehart Road
Lake Mary, Florida 32746
www.siloam.com

Unless otherwise noted, all Scripture quotations are from the Holy Bible, New Living Translation, copyright © 1996. Used by permission of Tyndale House Publishers, Inc., Wheaton, IL 60189.

Scripture quotations marked KJV are from the King James Version of the Bible.

This book is not intended to take the place of medical advice and treatment from your personal physician. Readers are advised to consult their own doctor or other qualified health professional regarding the treatment of their medical problems. Neither the publisher nor the author takes any responsibility for any possible consequences from any treatment, action or application of medicine supplement, herb or preparation to any person reading or following the information in this book. If readers are taking prescription medications, they should consult with their physicians and not take themselves off of medicines to start supplementation without the proper supervision of a physician.

Library of Congress Catalog Card Number: 00-101182
International Standard Book Number: 1-59185-217-X

05 06 07 08 — 9 8 7 6 5 4 3
Printed in the United States of America

To my wife, Mary.
Thank you for your loving support,
input and enthusiasm, which helped
make this book possible.

And to my father and mother—
Don Colbert Sr. and Kitty Colbert—
for their ongoing love and support and
continued spiritual guidance.

Contents

INTRODUCTION

I WISH I HAD
KNOWN ABOUT...

J UST AFTER HIS thirty-eighth birthday, my friend Carmen* passed away from a heart attack.

He was a slender fellow who didn't smoke or drink; he looked to be a specimen of good health. Suddenly, without warning, he was gone.

I had known him for several years, yet we had never discussed health issues. How could someone in the prime of life pass from this earth so quickly? What was happening inside of this man that caused his heart attack?

One of the reasons I have written this book is because of my conviction that Carmen would be alive today if he had read and followed the advice on these pages.

---

* Not his real name.

ARMED WITH KNOWLEDGE

I WISH YOU could step into my shoes for just one week. You would be heartbroken because of the sickness and disease that devastate so many lives.

What do you say to a twenty-seven-year-old man who has congestive heart failure? How do you tell parents that their child has a life-threatening illness?

I recently spoke with a woman, age thirty-four, who has colon cancer. A team of surgeons had done their best to remove the growth, yet it was spreading in her body. The woman was rather surprised when I asked, "How often do you have a bowel movement?"

She hesitated, then replied, "Oh, about once or twice a week." Then she asked, "But what does that have to do with anything?"

"It has everything to do with your health and recovery," I told her. It probably was one of the major reasons why she developed colon cancer in the first place.

Our nation may have the most highly trained surgeons, the finest hospitals and the most sophisticated equipment, yet the average person doesn't have a clue about basic health and nutrition. Millions are dying because of ignorance. In the case of the thirty-four-year-old woman with colon cancer, what she *didn't* know was killing her.

PREVENTION OR TREATMENT?

MEDICALLY, THIS IS the greatest time in the history of our planet. It's tragic, however, that we wait until a person is either sick or has serious symptoms to use the marvelous diagnostic tools available. People—and their insurance companies—spend incredible amounts of money on operations for heart bypasses, liver transplants and cancer surgeries. However, much of the enormous cost involved could be avoided if people would be proactive and follow some simple rules for health.

We have built model medical institutions, yet it seems their foundations rest on a bed of sand rather than on solid rock. Sadly, many have concluded that the health industry is based on treatment rather than prevention.

Where is the passion to attack the root causes of the world's health problems? Other than in nutritional medical circles, where is the deep concern for drinking pure water, eating wholesome foods and breathing clean air?

You are about to be armed with significant knowledge about our toxic environment.

- What dangerous chemicals are we ingesting from everyday foods?
- How can we eliminate the dangers from the water we drink?
- How can we detoxify our bodies without causing additional harm?
- What are the dangers and benefits of fasting?
- What vitamin and mineral supplements are necessary?
- What foods contain the vital nutrients we need?

OVERWORKED
AND UNDERNOURISHED

I CONTINUALLY MEET people who complain, "Dr. Colbert, I'm absolutely drained. When I get home from work all I want to do is lie down and go to bed."

The problem we face is not necessarily that we are overworked—it's that we are undernourished!

You will learn the foods you need to ingest for renewed strength and vivacious energy. I believe the dietary and lifestyle changes you will make because of this information will cause you to be renewed and invigorated.

WHO'S AT FAULT?

AFTER MANY YEARS in the medical field I have concluded that most sickness is self-inflicted—either by willful, destructive habits or by ignorance. Isn't it time that we take the responsibility for prevention of disease rather than for treatment? Think of the agony that would be avoided.

WONDERFULLY MADE

YOUR BODY IS an amazing creation—something far superior to anything developed by man. Only God Himself could have created such a remarkable work of art. We not only have a body that functions with billions of parts, but we are also blessed with feelings and emotions. The psalmist wrote, "Thank you for making me so wonderfully complex! Your workmanship is marvelous— and how well I know it" (Ps. 139:14).

You were not placed on earth to be anemic, feeble and helpless. God wants you to live "more abundantly"—disease free and in maximum health.

I want you to view this book as an "owner's manual" that will help to keep your body in good repair. You need to know when to change your oil, when to clean your radiator and how to make sure every cylinder is working at the highest capacity.

Please don't wait until you have a medical emergency. Start immediately to build a vibrant, healthy body—the younger the better.

On these pages you will discover:

- The menace you face from mercury
- How a shortage of water affects your health
- Steps you can take to detoxify your body
- The threats you face from cadmium, lead and aluminum
- Dangerous toxins and how to counter them
- How emotions affect your immune system
- How to remake your body with live foods
- The dangers of sugar
- The keys to proper digestion
- What you should know about milk and meat
- How to replace depleted nutrients in your body
- How to find the essential minerals for life
- The causes and cures of physical fatigue
- How to protect enzymes and cells
- How to use antioxidants to fight disease
- How to counter the causes of aging
- How to protect yourself from free radicals
- What you need to know about colloidal minerals
- What you can do about oxygen deprivation
- How to counter the "silent invaders" that are destroying your body

TWENTY YEARS FROM NOW

AT A RECENT medical seminar in Miami, I walked into a conference room filled with physicians. It was about eight o'clock in the morning, and a light buffet breakfast was being served.

We were there to learn the latest advances in health, yet you would not have been impressed with the eating habits of my colleagues. They were munching on sweet pastries and doughnuts, and stirring cream and sugar in their caffeinated coffee.

Out of the corner of my eye I noticed a physician walking toward the buffet table. He was a tall, slender man—about forty-five to fifty years of age. Just after he filled his bowl with cereal, he reached into his pocket and pulled out a small envelope and poured the contents on the cereal. Then he closed the envelope and put it back into his pocket, thinking no one had seen him.

Not being shy, I walked over to the doctor and inquired, "May I ask what you pulled out of your pocket? What did you put on your cereal?"

"Oh, this is just fiber," he smiled. "It's something I have been doing for nearly twenty years."

We introduced ourselves, and the physician told me about a lecture he had heard two decades earlier. "Dr. Dennis Burkett, a rather famous British physician, gave an incredible lecture on fiber," he said. "I've never forgotten it, and I am still following his advice. I carry a little packet of fiber with me everywhere I go. I wouldn't start the day without it."

What impressed me about this doctor was that he had heard the lecture twenty years ago and was still following the advice.

I would be thrilled beyond words if you walked up to me twenty years from now and said, "Dr. Colbert, I read your book *What You Don't Know May Be Killing You,* and I'm still practicing the principles I learned."

That is my desire for you.

1

THE MENACE
OF MERCURY

IF I CAME into the room in which you're sitting and broke open a vial of mercury and poured it on the floor, you might be told to evacuate the building while men in special contamination suits cleaned it up. That's how toxic mercury is. But I'll bet you didn't know that every time you chew your food you could be releasing mercury into your body.

Several years ago I suffered from a severe case of chronic fatigue and barely had enough energy to work. My skin looked terrible—it was a gray sallow color. People would ask, "Don, are you sick?"

"No, I'm not sick; I'm just tired," I would answer.

Almost every evening when I came home from work I'd go straight to bed, saying, "I'm exhausted. I've got to rest."

After much searching to determine the cause of my fatigue, I had a hair analysis, which revealed elevated mercury levels. An analysis of my urine also revealed a high mercury level.

Since mercury is widely present in the environment, nearly everyone may be exposed to low levels of mercury in the air, water and food. Not just a few individuals—*everyone!* However, some people may be exposed to higher levels of this dangerous toxin.

You are usually exposed to mercury in two ways. Many are endangered by eating fish, or shellfish, contaminated with methyl mercury. Some fish contain such high levels of mercury that selling them for human consumption has been prohibited. In certain areas, public health advisories have been issued by state and federal authorities discouraging anyone from catching fish destined for the dinner table. I recommend that you eat fish no more than three or four times a week.

The other most likely form of exposure to mercury is by absorbing mercury vapors released from dental fillings. What dental fillings? *The silver amalgam fillings.* Approximately one million of these mercury silver fillings are placed in the mouths of patients in the United States daily during the working week.

There is a lot of confusion about silver amalgam fillings. Dentists have been using mercury fillings for many years—in fact, more than 160 years.

Even though dentists have used them that long, controversy over their use has been around for about the same amount of time. Back in the 1840s, organized dentistry in the United States banned as unethical any dentist who used mercury in a patient. Today, although new research on the dangers of silver amalgam fillings is surfacing, the American Dental Association (ADA) still favors and supports the continued use of mercury silver amalgam fillings. With the amount of research available to alert dentists and patients alike to the dangers of amalgam, no doubt more and more people will discontinue the use of mercury fillings.

One dental practitioner in Colorado Springs tested over seven thousand patients and showed that over 90 percent of these patients demonstrated immune reactivity to low levels of mercury. This finding is very different from a survey taken in 1984, which showed that only 5 percent of the American population was sensitive to mercury fillings. Yet if 5 percent of our population had AIDS, over twelve million people would be affected—a very significant number of people. Do we continue to believe the earlier information from those who support the use of silver mercury amalgams (*which contain 50 percent mercury*), or do we believe the increasing scientific medical research and anecdotal evidence on living patients, which glaringly indicates that mercury fillings are unsafe?

For many years the dental community maintained that mercury was tightly bound with other metal components and did not escape from amalgam fillings. But research has proven that mercury vapors do escape during chewing, brushing and when contacted with hot or acidic food.

One study reported on levels of mercury vapor measured in the mouth after chewing. The mercury vapor level was fifty-four times higher in the mouth of an individual with amalgams than in the mouth of an individual without amalgams. It is physically impossible for mercury to be "locked in" the amalgam fillings once they are placed in the teeth.

The U.S. Department of Health and Human Services lists mercury as the third most toxic substance known to mankind.[1] There is no controversy over whether mercury is highly toxic. Mercury is more toxic than lead, cadmium and arsenic! At the International Conference on Biocompatibility of Materials held in 1988, a landmark conclusion for dentistry was made: "Based on the known toxic potentials of mercury and its documented release from dental amalgams, usage of mercury containing amalgam increases the health risk of the patients, the dentist and the dental personnel."

ARE YOUR MERCURY FILLINGS HARMING YOU?

DO YOU HAVE any amalgam fillings? Because of this ongoing controversy over mercury fillings, many dentists may tell you, "Don't worry about it. The problem is overblown."

Silver amalgam fillings are most likely your dentist's filling of choice, used by dentists the world over. Their color is silver, but over time, due to corrosion and chemical and electrical interaction, these fillings change to black, indicating the formation of mercurial salts—or tarnishing, as we know it. If your fillings have turned black, you may be in trouble. Many people who have mercury fillings experience a nasty metallic taste in their mouth. Do you?

Amalgam fillings contain a mixture of metals, composed of approximately 50 percent mercury, along with tin, silver, zinc and copper. Mercury, a well-known toxic heavy metal, has been scientifically proven unstable and has been shown to slowly bleed out of the amalgam filling. It finds a home inside the human body, mainly concentrating in the liver, kidneys, brain and endocrine glands. A recent study at the University of Tennessee showed mercury to be second only to radioactive plutonium on the toxic scale of inorganic heavy metals. A chronic, low-dose accumulation of toxic matter eventually puts stress on the immune system and may pollute the blood stream and every cell and organ in the body. Mercury has also been shown to cross the placenta and collect in fetal tissue. Studies show that the level of mercury in liver, kidney and brain tissue of a deceased fetus, newborn or young child is proportional to the number of amalgam fillings in the mother's mouth. In patients studied who had amalgam fillings for a period of time, more than 25 percent of the mercury was missing from amalgam fillings after five years!

The American Dental Association endorses mercury removal only in cases of cracks, chips, leaks or other structural problems. In my opinion this raises the question as to why. Why is the second most toxic metal on earth still the most common material used to fill teeth today?

I believe one of the reasons the ADA still supports amalgam fillings is because of the possible threats of lawsuits, which could affect them similarly to the tobacco industry. If the individual dentist recommends removal of amalgam fillings for reasons other than structural, he could face stiff fines or even the loss of his license to practice dentistry.

"I Just Don't Feel Good"

HEAVY METAL TOXICITY (as occurs in the slow release of mercury from amalgam fillings) is very slow. Usually the victims simply feel bad. They may say, "I don't know what is wrong with me—I just don't feel good, and I am very tired."

Mercury can induce an autoimmune response from your body's immune system. How does this happen? When mercury enters the membrane of a cell, the body's immune and surveillance systems may say that these are abnormal cells that must be dealt with. The immune system may then form antibodies against the seemingly abnormal cells (which appear abnormal because they contain mercury). The immune system defends the body by forming antibodies against the body's own cells, which can lead to rheumatoid arthritis, Hashimoto's thyroiditis, multiple sclerosis, lupus and other autoimmune diseases.

Autoimmune is when the immune system attacks itself, a process similar to a military disaster called "friendly fire." During Desert Storm, casualties occurred from troops firing on each other by accident—causing some of our troops to die. Autoimmune diseases are similar, and I believe mercury is a major contributor to these diseases.

Whether or not mercury silver fillings cause specific diseases is an important issue facing medical researchers today. Mercury exposure from any source and in any amount will usually cause mercury poisoning to some extent. Mercury, which is more toxic than lead or arsenic, may cause cell damage, death or irreversible chemical damage well before visible symptoms occur.

THE EFFECTS OF MERCURY POISONING

THERE IS SCIENTIFIC evidence to show how mercury, once it reaches its destination of a tissue or cell, expresses its toxicity. Mercury has the following effects upon the body:

- It inhibits DNA repair.
- It alters the cell's ability to control the exchange of materials coming into and going out of the cell.
- It can alter the specific arrangements of atoms within a molecule (the tertiary structure of molecules), thus producing a nonfunctional chemical.
- It can hinder the function of enzymes.
- It interferes with nerve impulses.
- It produces autoimmune responses.
- It interferes with endocrine function.
- It displaces other good minerals in the body.
- It can kill or alter digestive bacteria.
- It can contribute to antibiotic resistance.

What Are the Symptoms of Mercury Exposure?

Mercury can cause a variety of seemingly unrelated symptoms. Many of these are nonspecific and could easily be misdiagnosed as having resulted from other environmental contaminants or medical conditions. For that reason, mercury exposure has been called the "great masquerader." Some of the symptoms that may be associated with mercury exposure include:

- Tremors in fine voluntary muscle movements, such as handwriting
- Depression, fatigue, increased irritability, moodiness and nervous excitability
- Inability to concentrate and loss of memory
- Insomnia or drowsiness
- Nausea and diarrhea
- Loss of appetite
- Birth defects and miscarriages
- Nephritis or symptoms of kidney disease
- Pneumonitis
- Swollen glands and tongue
- Ulceration of oral mucosa
- Sores and ulcers in the mouth
- Dark pigmentation of gums and loosening of teeth

Excess mercury destroys cells by interfering with their ability to exchange nutrients, by hindering their ability to excrete waste and by decreasing oxygen that's needed by the cells. In other words, food and environmental allergies or sensitivities make the cell so *constipated* that it can't effectively take in nutrients or excrete waste—or even take in oxygen at a high level.

What is the result? For many people, their skin begins to turn gray and starts to sag. A doctor, looking under their tongue, usually sees dark blue or purple blood vessels instead of the normal, healthy, pink vessels. Nails that should be nice and shiny are dull, and the lunula, which are the "half moons" at the base of the nail, may have disappeared. Your fingernails are the windows of your body.

When I was mercury-toxic, only my thumbs had lunula. Since I've detoxified, all my half moons have returned on my fingers except on my little fingers. (You're not supposed to have one on your little finger.) This alone is not always a sign of mercury poisoning, yet it is common.

There is also concern that mercury leads to memory problems— often termed "mercury fog." It can impede the nerve cells' excretory system—the nerve cells can't get the nutrients in or expel the waste out. The resulting "fog" can trigger loss of memory.

Elevated mercury can also deactivate hormones. Many with low thyroid or low body temperature actually have too much mercury in their body, which is deactivating their thyroid hormone. In medical terms, studies have shown it inhibits the conversion of *T4* (the thyroid hormone tetraiodothyronine) to *T3* (the thyroid hormone triiodothyronine).

People with this condition may gain weight and have dry skin. Also, their hands are usually cold. It can affect the nerves, causing tingling and numbness. Plus, it can lead to chronic fatigue by blocking the oxygen binding to the hemoglobin. Mercury can also interfere with the female hormone *progesterone,* causing a decrease in sex drive and altering the menstrual cycles.

If you have concerns about any of these symptoms that you may be experiencing, my advice is to discuss the matter with a well-informed nutritional medical doctor who knows how to diagnose mercury toxicity. Call the American College for Advancement in Medicine (ACAM) at 1-800-LEADOUT to find a doctor near you.

There may be no need to rush into the costly project of having all of your fillings replaced immediately. In fact, I recommend nutritional supplementation for a few months prior to replacing fillings. You may want to have one filling or one quadrant replaced every few months or at least once a year.

BETTER TO BE SAFE THAN SORRY

BASED ON AVAILABLE scientific research and on my own research into this issue, without hesitation I tell patients not to allow any dentist to put silver amalgam fillings in their mouths.

Pregnant women should avoid having any silver fillings placed in their mouths or taken out during their pregnancy. Why? Mercury can be transferred through the placenta to the fetus and produce a myriad of toxic effects, from learning disabilities to mental retardation.

When I discovered that I was mercury-toxic, my attack on my problem was twofold. First, I went through a special mercury detoxification regimen to begin binding the mercury and to strengthen my immune system by using vitamins, minerals, amino acids, chlorella (a form of algae), garlic and other supplements. Next, I had the eight large amalgam fillings in my mouth taken out and replaced with porcelain. It was both the detoxification program and the removal of the fillings that made a significant difference. My renewed energy level was astounding.

Mercury toxicity can hinder the body's ability to perspire, which in turn reduces the release of toxins. Several years earlier I had noticed that my sweat glands had virtually stopped working, and my skin color had become sallow. When I ran or worked out in the gym, I didn't sweat. At first I thought, *This is pretty cool. I'm in good shape.* I didn't know the danger I was in—my body was toxic.

This was a serious matter. Our skin is called "the third kidney" because sweat is almost the same composition as urine.

After the mercury detox and removal of my silver fillings, my skin color returned to normal, and I started perspiring again.

"WHAT DO I DO ABOUT THE FILLINGS I HAVE?"

WHAT IS THE most important factor to consider if you have silver amalgam dental fillings? Certainly do not run out and have your fillings just "ground out." Because of the dangers of mercury vapors, many dentists have shared horror stories about patients who have had their fillings removed and report that they are in worse shape than ever after the fillings have been removed.

There is a proper and safe way to have these fillings removed. Begin by finding a willing and cooperative biological dentist who is aware of the risks of mercury and is knowledgeable in the proper protocols for removing silver amalgam fillings.

Determining the results of low-dose mercury exposure is very difficult. No one laboratory test is 100 percent accurate, but medical laboratory and clinical testing will help to:

- Evaluate your overall health condition
- Identify other medical factors
- Identify lifestyle factors that may need modification
- Determine the need for therapeutic intervention
- Monitor organ performance (liver and kidney)
- Track mercury excretion from the body

Your physician may also want to do hormonal testing to determine if mercury has caused any hormonal disturbances. It is sometimes wise to test the functioning of the thyroid in patients experiencing coldness and fatigue. Progesterone, estrogen, testosterone and thyroid hormones are easy targets for mercury toxicity.

16

In addition to the testing, a comprehensive patient health history and physical exam are, of course, necessities. It will probably be necessary for your medical doctor or dentist to conduct a serum compatibility test for you.

When you have found a competent biological dentist, he will probably begin the process of determining how best to treat your mercury toxicity. He may use a controlled chewing test to determine the extent of mercury being released from your dental fillings daily. He may conduct electrical readings on your fillings to determine the "sequence" for removing fillings, perhaps removing the negatively charged fillings first. To find a biological dentist, call the International College of Integrative Medicine (formerly Great Lakes College of Clinical Medicine) at 1-866-464-5226, or visit their Web site at www.glccm.org.

During the removal of amalgam, the patient can be exposed to amounts of mercury that are a thousand times greater than the EPA allowable concentration. It will probably be necessary for the biological dentist to conduct a serum compatibility test. Just because a certain type of filling has no mercury does not mean that your body will be compatible with it. Many plastic filling materials contain aluminum, toluene, acylates, acetates, antimony and a host of other materials that can create adverse reactions. This testing to determine what may be best suited for you, using cutting-edge technology based upon research, will be vitally important.

Your medical doctor may want to do blood testing to screen and select the appropriate nutritional program for you. This would be considered as true preventive nutrition. With the proper nutritional program in effect both before and after your fillings are removed, you should begin to feel healthier with noticeable changes in your appearance and energy level.

SAFE REMOVAL OF MERCURY FILLINGS

WHEN YOUR DOCTOR has completed his testing and evaluated the results, you and he together will determine what course of treatment to pursue. If you decide to go ahead and have your mercury fillings removed, it must be done with extreme caution. It will be important to consider both your own protection as the patient and the protection of the dentist and his staff. A good biological dentist will follow all the necessary precautions for safety—for the patients and the staff.

IMPORTANT LIFESTYLE CHANGES FOR YOUR HEALTH

ONCE YOU HAVE taken the necessary steps to detoxify your body of mercury toxins, you will want to make any necessary changes to continue to reduce your intake of mercury and increase the excretion rate of mercury. Even if, with your doctor's counsel, you do not find it crucial to remove any fillings you may have, you will still want to reduce your intake of mercury and other toxins.

DIETARY CONSIDERATIONS

THE LARGEST DIETARY source of mercury comes from fish and fish products. There is an important message that everyone should know about the risks of mercury in fish. Although fish are an important part of a balanced diet, there are underlying risks associated with its consumption. Some species of fish may contain higher levels of mercury.

The Center for Food Safety and Applied Nutrition and the U.S. Food and Drug Administration have both issued statements for pregnant women, nursing mothers and women of childbearing age who may become pregnant. Studies indicate that methyl mercury may damage an unborn child's developing nervous system if eaten regularly. Women are advised to protect their unborn child by being more selective when choosing the fish that they eat.[2]

In the United States, the limit for methyl mercury in commercial marine and freshwater fish is 1.0 parts per million (ppm). Mercury levels of the most commonly consumed fish and seafood are normally below these limits. However, some species often do exceed 1.0 ppm. Fish with high levels of methyl mercury are white snapper, swordfish, king mackerel, shark, tilefish and tuna steak. Older fish and large fish that eat other fish tend to have the most mercury. If you catch fish, check to see if there is a fish advisory in your area that will enable you to be aware of posted warnings. Fish is a healthy food if you choose wisely.

HEALTHY LIMITS FOR SEAFOOD CONSUMPTION

According to the Washington State Department of Health and the Food and Drug Administration, pregnant women, nursing mothers and women of childbearing age should limit the amount of canned tuna they eat to about one can, or six ounces, per week. Other recommendations are to limit tuna steaks, halibut and orange roughy to once a month. Cod, pollack, haddock and tuna should be eaten only once a week, and salmon and shellfish should be limited to two to three meals per week.

SOMETHING TO CONSIDER

If the Center for Food Safety and Applied Nutrition and the U.S. Food and Drug Administration have both issued a warning to women about the effects of mercury consumption, perhaps every man, woman and child should heed the same warning. Research indicates that you can safely eat approximately 12 ounces of cooked fish per week. A typical serving would be anywhere from 3 to 6 ounces. Of course, eating smaller portions of fish would allow you the pleasure of increasing the number of times you consume it each week.

NUTRITIONAL HELP

Pork and fatty cuts of red meat should also be eliminated from the diet during detoxification.

To enhance excretion of mercury and other toxic metals, increase fiber intake to 30–40 grams per day. You can get your fiber naturally from raw fruits, vegetables, salads, legumes, beans and grains. A high-fiber diet reduces the amount of time that foods and liquids containing heavy metals remain in the colon. Avoid constipation during detoxification. Eat unsweetened yogurt to assist in the maintenance of your intestinal flora, or take Lactobacillis acidophilus and bifidus.

Drink a minimum of two quarts of filtered water daily. A gallon of water daily is the preferred intake. It is recommended that coffee or caffeine products be eliminated or drastically reduced. Make every effort to reduce the amount of stress to which you are normally subjected. Get adequate rest each night, as your immune system will be stressed during a detoxification procedure.

If you are not exercising, establish some schedule of physical exercise at least three times a week for thirty minutes each time. I would also recommend that you utilize a sauna, or even better, an infrared sauna, as sweating helps to eliminate toxic metals. But start out slowly, five to ten minutes only, at a low temperature. Infrared saunas are better for detoxifying mercury and other toxins. Give up chewing gum until all amalgam fillings have been replaced. Chewing gum causes the release of mercury vapor from amalgams.

SUPPLEMENTATION

Supplements can be used to correct deficiencies and to enhance your immune system. The more toxic metals you have taken into your body, the greater the need for nutrients just to protect the cells from harm. Many of the nutrients I recommend have the ability to bind with mercury, lead and other toxic metals, thus reducing the burden upon your body.

The presence of heavy metals in your body causes the formation of free radicals. Even though your body has a defense system against free radicals, supplements that are antioxidants can increase the body's natural defense system's ability to reduce the cell-damaging effect of free radicals.

During the process of detoxification, your muscles may "feel" less energetic and even weak. It is very important to avoid stimulants of any kind to abort this process. Some of the symptoms you may experience as a result of the detoxification process are headaches, fever/chills, colds, skin eruptions, constipation, diarrhea, fatigue/ sluggishness, nervousness, irritability, depression, frequent urination and others. These are usually signs that your body is becoming healthier as it eliminates waste and toxins. As the body cleanses, each reaction becomes milder and shorter in duration, followed by longer and longer periods of feeling better than ever before, until you reach a level plateau of vibrant health.

The following list shows supplements that current nutritional research has indicated may be of benefit during a detoxification program. Take only the ones your healthcare provider or doctor has recommended as absolutely necessary.

- DL-methionine (Redoxal HMF)—DL-methionine and metabolites help the body detoxify heavy metals, including mercury, chemicals, pesticides, herbicides and xenobiotics. L-methionine inhibits toxic metals from crossing the blood-brain barrier. In other words, it prevents metal ions such as methyl mercury, which are attached to other l-form amino acids, from crossing the blood-brain barrier and depositing mercury and other metals into the brain. It is recommended that you take one capsule of Redoxal (dl-methionine) three times a day in the beginning, at least two weeks before the first amalgam removal, and that you continue at least six months after the last amalgam is removed. (See Appendix for ordering information.)

· A chelated multivitamin and multimineral (such as Divine Health Multivitamins)—to provide adequate vitamins and minerals to replace those that are displaced by the mercury, including zinc, selenium and magnesium. Take three tablets with your morning and evening meals, for a total of six.

· Chlorella—this all-natural freshwater algae is one of the most potent whole foods on earth. It has been proven to assist the body in detoxifying heavy metals like mercury, lead and cadmium. Begin with three capsules daily, and increase gradually until taking nine capsules daily.

· Garlic—a natural substance that is a strong chelator of toxic metals. Take 500 milligrams three times a day.

· Vitamin C—use a "buffered form" such as Divine Health Buffered Vitamin C, one capsule three times a day. You can order from our Web site at www.drcolbert.com.

· Antioxidant formula—that contains a comprehensive selection of antioxidants to limit free-radical formation. This formula should include vitamin C, vitamin E, beta carotene, coenzyme Q_{10}, vitamin A, lipoic acid, grape seed extract and pine bark extract. Divine Health Elite

Antioxidant and Divine Health Multivitamins contain all of these powerful antioxidants. Take one capsule three times a day.

· Liver detoxification formula (such as Divine Health Milk Thistle)—in order for the liver to function properly, it must be protected from toxic buildup and cleansed periodically. Milk thistle is very important for supporting proper liver function.

· MSM—is an organic form of sulfur that is in a very bioavailable form. It is found naturally in whole grains, vegetables and legumes. It is also found in animal protein such as meat, poultry, milk and eggs. MSM, however, can be destroyed in cooking and processing. Also, many of our soils are depleted in sulfur. Many patients with mercury toxicity are deficient in sulfur since mercury deprives the body of sulfur. I recommend Divine Health MSM, one tablet two to three times a day.

· DMSA—an oral chelating agent I use to perform urine challenge testing to test for mercury toxicity after amalgams are removed. Usually mercury levels are elevated in the urine. I place patients on DMSA for three days in order to remove mercury from their body, and then I stop the chelation for eleven days. I continue this cycle for a few months and then recheck the urine challenge test. I also monitor their blood work and urine every four to eight weeks. DMSA is available only with a prescription.

To enhance removal of mercury, I recommend using an infrared sauna. Sauna therapy helps the body release mercury.

(See Appendix to order.) Also, avoid stress and get plenty of rest, as you will more than likely experience increased fatigue.

To enhance toxin removal, soak for thirty minutes in a tub of warm water with 2 to 4 cups of Epsom salts three times weekly. Avoid stress, and get plenty of rest as you will more than likely experience increased fatigue.

LIVING IN CONTINUED GOOD HEALTH

DON'T IGNORE THE mercury levels in your body. Your life may depend on it. When you have taken all the necessary steps to detoxify your body of mercury and all other toxins, you will have much more energy, your mind will be sharper, you will be in better physical shape, and your health depends on it.

I recommend that you maintain your new healthy lifestyle for the rest of your life! Begin to end the menace of mercury today!

DR. COLBERT'S CHECKLIST
FOR MERCURY

-√ Mercury is highly toxic.

-√ Mercury may induce an autoimmune response leading to lupus, rheumatoid arthritis, multiple sclerosis or thyroiditis.

-√ Mercury displaces other good minerals from your body.

-√ Pregnant women should avoid any silver fillings being placed in their mouths or taken out during pregnancy.

-√ Find a competent biological dentist to determine how best to treat your mercury toxicity.

-√ During the removal of amalgam, you can be exposed to amounts of mercury that are a thousand times greater than the EPA allowable concentration. So be sure your dentist knows how to employ the special precautions necessary during the removal of the filling.

-√ Do not allow a dentist to put in amalgam fillings; ask for porcelain fillings instead.

-√ Find a dentist who practices "mercury-free dentistry."

-√ Fish that are lowest in mercury content include sardines, herring, pollack, mackerel, cod, red fish and Greenland halibut.

-√ Limit your consumption of lobster, shrimp and tuna. They may contain high amounts of heavy metals.

2

THE DEBACLE
OF DEHYDRATION

ONE OF THE most incredible things about visiting Alaska is the unspoiled environment. The air is wonderfully fresh and the water pristine. It's like no water you've tasted here in the continental United States. It makes you wonder what the Garden of Eden was like. The water that flowed through it must have been delightful, crystal clear and wonderfully pure.

Compared to our daily tap water, well, it's no wonder so many of us find it difficult to drink enough water. However, what you don't know about drinking enough water might be killing you.

At a health seminar I recently conducted, someone asked, "Dr. Colbert, what is the most important nutrient in our body?"

Without hesitation I answered, "Water!" It's the main transport media of the body that delivers nutrients to all the cells. It is also essential to digestion—helping us absorb, assimilate and eliminate. Your body can exist for about five weeks without food, but the average person can only live about five days without water.

Here are some amazing facts about water:

- Your body is about 60 percent water.
- Your muscles are about 75 percent water.
- Your brain is about 75 percent water.
- Your blood is approximately 82 percent water.
- Your bones are approximately 25 percent water.

Few people realize that the average-sized human requires about three quarts of water a day. (To determine your water needs, take your body weight in pounds and divide it by 2. This will equal the amount of water in ounces that you need per day. For example, a 200-pound man needs 100 ounces of water a day: 200 divided by 2 equals 100 ounces.)

To help you visualize this, the next time you look at a one-gallon container of milk, imagine it three-quarters full. That's about how much water your body needs *daily*. Yet it is disturbing to me to know that most people do not drink *one* cup of water a day, let alone three quarts—the amount they truly need.

You say, "That's a large quantity. I could never drink that much!"

Fortunately, you are already one-third of the way toward the objective simply by the foods you eat. You absorb about one quart of water in your daily routine. For example, bananas are over 70 percent water, apples are 80 percent water and tomatoes are approximately 95 percent water.

The next time you visit the zoo and see a huge gorilla, you won't find him at a drinking fountain, yet he is getting his daily liquid requirements from the large quantities of food he ingests. You may ask, "What about an order of toast, a fast-food hamburger, a baked potato or a piece of apple pie? Don't they count?"

Unfortunately, starchy processed foods, cooked meats and most fats contain very little water. So if these are your main food sources, your intake is deficient. However, if you are eating plenty of fruits and vegetables, you're likely getting your one-quart minimum. Remember, in addition to your food, you need two extra quarts of water—and if you live in a warm climate, a little more.

A women recently told me, "I'm not really concerned. I drink at least two or three quarts of iced tea a day—that should give me my requirement."

Coffee, tea and sodas are caffeinated beverages. They do not meet your water requirements, for caffeine is a diuretic and actually causes you to *lose* water.

THE DEFICIT DANGER

HAVE YOU EVER heard a weatherman give this weather report? "Friends, we need some rain. We are nine inches short of the average rainfall so far this year. Consequently, crops are failing and trees are dying because of this shortage."

Do you realize the same thing can be happening to you because you are "water deficient"? What is the result of not drinking enough water? You won't have sufficient fluid in your tissues, and you may become chronically dehydrated.

Once, when I was explaining the need for water to a patient, he said, "I don't think I have a problem. I would have a dry mouth if this were the case."

I explained to him that a dry mouth is one of the last signs of dehydration. As a resident of Florida, I've lived through several periods of water rationing. When we don't receive adequate amounts of rainfall, the government takes action. For example, washing your car is prohibited, and you can't water your lawn during the day—only in the evening and sometimes not at all.

That's what our body does when we become chronically dehydrated: It begins to ration our water. If the warning signals are ignored and we don't give our bodies the liquids they need, serious problems begin to surface. To be specific, we can begin to develop rectal diseases—irritable bowel, diverticulosis, chronic constipation and hemorrhoids.

Lack of this vital element also contributes to varicose veins, heart disease, high blood pressure, asthma, allergies, hiatal hernias, ulcers, arthritis, back and neck pain, headaches, memory loss, high cholesterol and even kidney stones.

A Cry for Help

HERE'S WHY AN adequate supply of water is critical. Every function of the body is related to the flow of blood that carries nutrients, hormones and other elements to the tissues. The nutrients first go to the vital organs: your brain, heart, kidneys, liver and lungs.

Follow this closely. The shortage of intake will cause loss of water volume in the cells, which affects the efficiency of delivering nutrients and excreting waste products. What is the result? We don't have enough nutrients in the cells, and we have more waste collecting in those same cells.

Imagine that the symptoms occurring from chronic dehydration are expressed by the body's crying out, "Help! I'm thirsty. I desperately need water!"

For most people, the symptoms are detected by their doctor. However, instead of treating the patient with water, the physician often writes out a prescription, and you (the patient) rush to your nearest pharmacy. The medicine turns your "signal for help" off and temporarily delays your cry for water. Almost without noticing, you become trapped in a cycle that grows worse and worse. You take a pill for one condition, and something else starts failing. You get a prescription for that, and a third symptom occurs.

I cannot count the people who have come to my office with a list of twenty or thirty different drugs they are taking—medications that are simply suppressing symptoms.

The information in this book is to prevent you from needing these drugs. Why? Because once you begin, it is a vicious cycle—one that is difficult to stop. Over time, your kidneys may not function as well, and you may find yourself in a position where you *must* take the drugs.

THE VITAL CONNECTION

TO BETTER UNDERSTAND the essential connection between water and good health, let's look at six common conditions.

1. ARTHRITIS

At some point in life almost everyone is affected by arthritis or neck and back pain.

Back or neck pain may be caused by disks wearing out due to inadequate fluid within the disk. Our backs have disks between the vertebral bones that are made up of a fibrous material called the *anulus fibrosus.* This is filled with a jelly-like substance called the *nucleus pulposus.* As much as 75 percent of the weight of our upper body is supported by the nucleus pulposus, which is the fluid inside that disk. Only 25 percent of our upper body weight is supported by the anulus fibrosus. Therefore, when our disks become dehydrated they are more prone to herniate and develop degenerative disk disease or arthritis.

It's similar to driving a car on a nearly flat tire. Over time the tire is going to wear out and perhaps even blow. It is the same with your disks. If you stay in a state of dehydration for a significant period of time, you're headed for a serious breakdown.

Cartilage provides the smooth surface so that joints can glide easily during movement. Cartilage is about five times slicker than ice, and cartilage is about 80 percent water. As long as the cartilage is well hydrated, there is minimal frictional forces, and the joint will remain healthy. However, if the cartilage is dehydrated, there will be increased frictional forces and thus more damage to the cartilage, leading to arthritis.

Avoiding arthritic conditions is just one of the important reasons to drink two quarts of water every day. It's preventive medicine.

2. HIGH BLOOD PRESSURE

Earlier we indicated that the body rations water to make certain the vital organs (the brain, heart, kidneys, liver and lungs) receive it first. However, when that happens, the flow of water may be constricted to other areas of the body in order to pump blood to these vital areas first. What is the result? Your arteries may eventually become constricted, driving your blood pressure up.

I'm sure you have noticed that when you constrict a water hose, it actually increases the water pressure. That's similar to how our arteries behave. Simply by increasing our intake of water, we help to open up our arteries, thus preventing a rise in blood pressure. When a person has high blood pressure, he is given medication to open up or dilate these vital passageways. I am convinced that the best treatment available is *water*.

If high blood pressure is detected early enough, drinking two to three quarts of water a day may reduce the pressure to normal.

Why do I say "detected early"? If the disease progresses to the point that your kidneys suffer damage, they will not filter properly. In such cases, drinking two to three quarts a day may actually cause edema, which is *swelling*. It is important to start this process early to avoid becoming dependent on medication.

3. HIATAL HERNIAS

In my residency program early in my medical career, I delivered about two hundred babies. I noticed that when women were between seven and nine months pregnant they would almost always develop a hiatal hernia—the protrusion of the stomach up through the diaphragm. This happened because the growing baby caused the uterus to push against the stomach. When these women would lie down, stomach acid would run up, and they would experience heartburn, indigestion and hiatal hernia symptoms. But when they delivered the baby, all the symptoms would usually disappear.

Today, I see middle-aged men and women walking around who look as if they are nine months pregnant because of the weight they are carrying. Their stomachs are being pushed up through the diaphragm, and we are seeing hiatal hernias because of the weight and increased pressure.

The two best treatments for this condition are meeting your daily water-intake needs and following a weight-loss program. However, do not drink water for three to four hours prior to bedtime, because acid reflux disease is commonly associated with a hiatal hernia. Thus, water prior to bedtime may reflux up and cause heartburn.

4. ULCERS

Few people realize that maintaining the proper water level can greatly relieve ulcer disease.

The person who is not drinking the needed two quarts of water daily is existing in a water-deficit state. Stop to think again about the body's rationing program, which delivers the precious liquid to vital organs. When a person is water deficit, because the body rations the water to our vital organs first, there may not be enough left to rehydrate the mucous layer in our stomach, which is 98 percent water. The mucous layer protects us against stomach acid. The layer also contains bicarbonate, which neutralizes the stomach acid. When we drink water, the mucous layer becomes much thicker, preventing the acid from burning the stomach lining.

Remember, it's water, not expensive medicine, that provides lasting relief from ulcers. Also, it is now proven that most ulcers are caused by bacteria called *Helicobacter pylori*. Low gastric acid output will encourage the growth of this bacteria. Most ulcer medications reduce or neutralize hydrochloric acid, thus encouraging the growth of the bacteria and creating a vicious cycle.

5. Asthma

Can water reduce the effects of asthma? Absolutely. Your bronchial tubes—the airways of your system—need water to have moisture in order to prevent constriction.

Asthmatics usually have elevated histamine levels. Histamine is a neurotransmitter that causes contraction of muscles in the bronchial tubes, leading to symptoms of asthma. Animal studies have shown that the production of histamine will decrease as water intake increases. Water is also an excellent treatment for allergies since allergies are also usually associated with elevated histamine levels.[1]

Elevated histamine causes itchy eyes, nasal draining and other allergic symptoms.

6. Alzheimer's disease

Can water reduce the risk of dementia and Alzheimer's disease?

Think for a moment about your brain. Now think about a plum. Without water it shrinks and becomes like a prune. In the brain, cells may become dehydrated due to lack of adequate hydration. Without adequate water, the brain may not obtain nourishment, and it may not be able to properly eliminate waste matter. Thus I believe that long-term dehydration may contribute to Alzheimer's disease. Remember, your brain is 75 percent water. Can you see why you should never allow it to become dehydrated?

For further information on the use of water to prevent and treat diseases, I strongly recommend the book *Your Body's Many Cries for Water* by Dr. F. Batmanghelidj.

AN ANTIAGING CURE?

LET ME ASK you two questions:

1. When we remove water from grapes, what do we have? Raisins.
2. When we remove water from our skin, what is the result? Wrinkles.

If for no other reason than to have smooth, glowing skin, you need to drink the minimum water requirement. It's a lesson many motion picture actors and popular stage performers learned decades ago. In a television interview that I watched, singer Tina Turner, while advancing in years, publicly attributed her youthful appearance to drinking at least two quarts of water every day. It is interesting to note that a great number of leaders in the entertainment industry practice natural medicine as opposed to prescription drugs.

THE TIMETABLE

YOU KNOW HOW much water you should drink, but when should you drink it?

The best time is when you wake up in the morning—about thirty minutes before breakfast. Start with an 8-ounce glass.

You may be wondering, *Can I have my usual glass of orange juice and tea or coffee with breakfast?* Sure. Don't let the addition of water to your diet put you in bondage. Orange juice is fine. If you feel you still need coffee or tea, drink it in moderation.

Next, drink another 8-ounce glass of water about two and a half hours after breakfast.

As you near lunch time, repeat your breakfast schedule. Thirty minutes before lunch have another 8-ounce glass—or *two* glasses if you will be having a big lunch.

Drinking water before meals has two important benefits:

1. **It will decrease your appetite because your stomach feels full.**
2. **It has a positive impact on your digestion.**

Perhaps you are looking at this routine and wondering, *What about drinking water with my meals? Wouldn't that be easier?*

It might seem practical, but it may not be beneficial. Here's why. When you have iced drinks or beverages with your meals—especially in large amounts—they can wash out the enzymes in your stomach and intestines. This delays digestion since the body must absorb the water first before the food. In this process, the temperature in the stomach heats up similar to a furnace. When you consume cold drinks with a meal, it's like pouring water on a fire and thus cooling down the heat necessary for digestion.

Yes, you can drink some water with a meal. That's what I usually order in a restaurant—bottled water with a slice of lemon. However, don't drink large amounts, but limit consumption to 4 to 8 ounces with a meal.

Two and one-half hours after lunch have another 8-ounce glass of water. Then thirty minutes before your evening meal drink your next glass.

Remember this: Before your largest meal of the day, either lunch or dinner, try drinking 16 ounces. I predict that you won't eat as much.

Finally, two and one-half hours after dinner have another 8-ounce glass and another before bedtime unless you have a hiatal hernia, reflux disease or an enlarged prostate. In those cases, do not drink anything else after dinner. If drinking water late in the evening causes you to get up during the night, simply increase your amounts before lunch and dinner.

Here's the recommended timetable for your 64 ounces (two quarts) of water each day.

30 minutes before breakfast:	8 ounces
2.5 hours after breakfast:	8 ounces
30 minutes before lunch:	8 ounces
2.5 hours after lunch:	8 ounces
30 minutes before dinner:	16 ounces
2.5 hours after dinner:	8 ounces
30 minutes before bedtime:	8 ounces

THE QUESTION OF QUALITY

I RECEIVED A letter recently from a man in California who was quite concerned. "Dr. Colbert," he wrote, "you're asking people to drink water, yet it's polluted with chemicals. Won't it do more harm than good?"

The gentleman has a valid point.

A great amount of the water flowing into our homes may have elevated levels of toxic chemicals. We need to be alert to the potential dangers.

There are two major chemicals being added to the water supply at municipal water treatment plants: chlorine and fluoride. However, don't pick up the phone and call the water company and ask, "Why are you putting these chemicals in my water?"

If chlorine was not added, bacteria remaining in the water would cause outbreaks of diarrhea among most water users. Chlorine kills most of the bacteria in the water—except for a few resistant parasites such as the parasite *Cryptosporidium*. These resistant parasites have caused disease outbreaks in several major cities.

There are also downsides to chlorine. For example, when a person takes a shower with chlorinated water, it can cause hair to become brittle and break off. It also contributes to dry skin.

How can you avoid the problem? Purchase a shower filter, which will remove 95 percent of chlorine from the water. I recommend the Wellness Shower Filter. (See Appendix for ordering information.)

You may wonder, *What about chlorine in the water I drink? Is it also dangerous?* Chlorine can destroy certain vitamins—including vitamins A, B, C and E, which are some of the main antioxidants protecting us against cancer and heart disease. It also can react with organic waste and form *trihalomethane*, a chemical that can cause cancer of the colon and bladder. In addition, when chlorine reacts with organic materials in water, it may increase your risk of developing allergies, asthma, kidney stones and atherosclerosis.

Recently I spoke with a nutritionist who operates three international cancer hospitals. Many of his patients are people who have been given up on by medical science.

"Dr. Colbert," he told me, "I believe two of the major factors contributing to most cancers are drinking chlorinated water and bathing and showering with chlorinated water." All of his patients drink filtered water and use shower filters. Clearly he believes that the use of chlorinated water may be more harmful than helpful. Perhaps we all need to take a closer look at this issue.

Do You Need Fluoride?

THE SECOND MAJOR chemical in our water supply is fluoride. It is added to prevent cavities and tooth decay, primarily in children.

Unfortunately, fluoride has been proven to partially inhibit more than one hundred different enzymes in the body. It can also interfere with vitamin and mineral functions, and it is linked to calcium deposits and arthritis. I believe a little fluoride in the water when we're forming teeth is fine. However, it isn't required when you reach your teen years or become an adult. Again, the use of a filter can help to eliminate this chemical.

THE SILENT INVADERS

THERE'S ANOTHER DANGER—toxic chemicals! I call these toxins *seepers,* since they may seep into our water supply. In many ways they are more dangerous than chlorine and fluoride, and they include chemicals from the air, industrial waste, pesticides, heavy metals and other pollutants.

If you believe that "what goes up must come down," you will understand the danger. What happens to the residue from industrial smokestacks, a detonated bomb or the pollution from automobiles? It eventually can find its way into our water supply.

A second source of seepers is industrial waste that pollutes our water. Just one discarded battery, leaking out mercury, lead or nickel cadmium, can place lives at risk.

According to Environmental Working Group (EWG), based in Washington, DC, manufacturers dumped more than one billion pounds of toxic chemicals into rivers, lakes and other bodies of water between 1990 and 1994. EWG also estimates that manufacturers contributed about 450 million additional pounds via sewage.[2]

In the 1940s, one billion pounds of synthetic chemicals were produced each year. By the 1980s, production was up to five hundred billion pounds. And one thousand new chemicals are introduced each year. Yet the Federal Safe Drinking Water Act addresses only one hundred contaminants.[3]

When I perform a hair analysis on a person, it is amazing what heavy metals the hair may contain. These metals include not just mercury and lead, but aluminum and even arsenic. Tests on one older gentleman revealed he had been exposed to tremendously high amounts of arsenic, probably from the water he had used.

Should we be concerned about toxic wastes from nuclear power plants, fertilizers, pesticides, petroleum products, bacteria, parasites, viruses and animal waste? Absolutely! They can be found as close as the water that flows from your kitchen sink.

It's logical to ask, "Doesn't my local water company filter out all these dangerous chemicals?" Oh, they operate within standards of public safety, but it is simply too expensive to totally block every dangerous toxin from reaching your home. After all, most of the supply is for nonhuman consumption such as watering lawns, washing clothes and flushing toilets.

Another kind of chemical that can be found in our water supply comes from pesticides and fertilizers that are used on plants and crops, which ultimately seep into the water supply. Unfortunately, most systems available do not totally filter out pesticides.

Two billion pounds of pesticides are used every year. That's eight pounds for every American. EWG found that a single glass of Midwestern tap water has three or more pesticides in it.[4]

According to the Environmental Working Group (EWG), farmers across the corn belt apply 150 million pounds of five herbicides: atrazine, cyanazine, simazine, alachorlor and metolachlor to their corn and soybean fields every spring. Rains wash a substantial portion of these chemicals into the drinking water of millions of people in the Midwest and Louisiana. These chemicals are not removed by the conventional municipal drinking water treatment technologies.[5]

Much of the nation's ground water and many of its streams are contaminated with pesticides and unhealthy levels of fertilizer chemicals. Surprisingly, some of the worst contamination by insecticides has been found in urban streams. And though banned in 1972, low levels of DDT turned up in stream sediment and fish in both urban and rural areas across the U.S. No one knows how combinations of contaminants at low levels affect human health or wildlife.[6]

Many pesticides contain neurotoxins that are toxic to the neurological system of the insect—and possibly toxic to us. Governments worldwide are wrestling with the issue of banning pesticides due to the rising levels of toxins that can be found in ground water. An effective water-treatment system would have to filter these neurotoxins down to parts per trillion—not million or billion, but *trillion*.

Environmental Working Group (EWG) tests show that the herbicide atrazine contaminates the tap water of almost ten million people in eight hundred cities and towns in the Midwest. In many places, children receive their lifetime dose of this carcinogen in their first four months.[7]

Mercury is found in thermometers, and a lot of people just break an old thermometer and throw it away. This mercury may eventually end up in our water supply.

That same mercury can find its way to our lakes. Soon small fish eat the algae containing the toxin. The small fish, in turn, are eaten by larger fish, which are caught and subsequently featured on the menu of a gourmet restaurant—fish that may contain high concentrations of dangerous mercury.

An outbreak of the microorganism cryptosporidium in Milwaukee's water supply in 1993 killed more than one hundred people and sickened another four hundred thousand. Such outbreaks threaten drinking water systems. Some believe that some outbreaks of intestinal flu may actually be caused by such microorganisms in drinking water.[8]

These toxins, and others, can be found in many of the water supplies throughout our nation and world. It would be easy to point a finger at the officials of our water treatment systems, yet the cost of total filtration is already too high—and taxpayers would vote down the exorbitant increases necessary for water that is absolutely pure.

We can't ignore the fact that toxins are plaguing our environment. We do not know to what extent compounds are leaching out of plastic bottles into our water. I have tried some bottled water that had a distinct chemical taste, and I believe it was due to chemical compounds leaching out of the plastic bottle. I never drank that brand of bottled water again.

Plastic bottles may contain hormone-disrupting chemicals that leach into the water. This may be one of the reasons there is a decreasing human male sperm count. It is best to use glass bottles. Discard any plastic bottle that, when opened, has a chemical odor, and avoid water in aluminum cans.

What Kind of Filter?

I believe it is imperative to have a good water-filter system in your home. To those who say, "I can't afford it," I respond, "Well, can you spend $10?" That's the cost of a water-filtering pitcher that will remove most of the chlorine and 90 percent of the lead. Yes, you will need to change the filter every few months, but it's better than nothing.

If you're still not convinced and continue to drink from your tap, at least let the water run for a few minutes every morning to remove the sediment. Let it run until the water is cool. Never drink hot water from your tap or use hot tap water in your cooking, because it leaches the metals out of the pipes.

You may wonder, *If I boil water, will it get rid of the chemicals?* No. Harmful bacteria may be killed, but the chemicals are still there. That's why you need to use filtered water for cooking and drinking.

You owe it to the health of your family to purchase a quality water filtration system. There are four main types of filters.

1. CARBON FILTERS

These are not only inexpensive, but they are also among the best filters on the market. They are by far the most common.

The two basic types of carbon filters are the granulated carbon block and the solid carbon block filter. They range in price from $50 to $100—with the cost of the solid block filter higher because it lasts longer. Granulated block filters are effective for three or four months before they need changing. The solid block filters last nearly one year.

I believe the solid block version is better than the granulated filter since it filters out nearly all microorganisms, including *Cryptosporidium.* It also will filter out chlorine, nearly 98 percent of lead, approximately 85 percent of mercury and most organic chemicals.

There is one caution to be aware of. Over time these filters (especially the granulated carbon filter) will collect sediment and bacteria and may actually breed bacteria. That's why it is essential to change the filters as recommended. You can't keep a carbon filter in use for years and say, "I'm filtering my water."

Carbon filters are not totally effective for heavy metals, and they will not remove fluoride. For $50 you can own a good filter. Activated carbon filters are excellent for removing VOCs (volatile organic chemicals) and trihalomethanes, which are carcinogens.

2. THE ALKALIZER

The Alkalizer filters by activated charcoal and then changes the water through an electrolysis process, creating alkaline water. This process produces two types of water: one is alkaline, which is used for consumption, and the other is acidic for external applications. Smaller mineral clusters are produced. The smaller cluster size gives the water excellent hydrating properties, high solubility and good permeability. Each of these waters has unique properties that can enhance the quality of our health.

3. REVERSE OSMOSIS

In my opinion, a reverse-osmosis system is one of the very best water filters on the market today. It removes chlorine, fluoride, bacteria, parasites, chemicals and heavy metals, including lead and mercury. It also eliminates most uranium, radium, strontium 90, pesticides including DDT, dieldrin, heptachlor, malathion and others. Reverse osmosis, however, does not adequately remove nitrates and trihalomethanes.

The cost is expensive—about $350 to $450. As a doctor, I believe this is a wise investment for your health.

I believe that the best water filters are the reverse-osmosis units with activated carbon filtration. However, the membranes of these filters must be changed regularly. Another excellent filter is a distiller that is combined with an activated carbon filter.

4. A WATER DISTILLER

Many people purchase water distillers that are extremely effective.

Certain volatile chemicals can vaporize and recondense, but many of the distillers have a carbon filter on top to trap those chemicals. The only way to get rid of the majority of pesticides is through *double* distillation—distilling the water twice. Distillation alone does not remove trihalomethanes or other volatile organic chemicals. Because they have a lower boiling point than water, they condense with the water.

There is a secondary benefit to distillation. Research shows that distilled water is beneficial to people who are prone to the development of kidney stones. However, I recommend a reverse-osmosis filter for most of my patients.

In addition to these major water-filtering systems, there are excellent shower filters. I believe that the Wellness Shower Filter is one of the best. It greatly reduces chlorine. Shower filters convert chlorine to safe chloride. As we discussed earlier, they greatly reduce the effect of chlorine on brittle hair and dry skin.

If you plan to store your filtered water for any length of time, it's best to use glass containers whenever possible. Plastic bottles can be treated with chemicals that can be absorbed by water over time.

BOTTLED WATER

USING BOTTLED WATER may be misleading, so read labels carefully. Bottled water is regulated, but not stringently. The only requirement placed on companies that dispense bottled water is that it is as safe as tap water. It may be nothing more than filtered tap water from some municipality. Many varieties of bottled water are very good, however. Just don't assume anything.[9]

Penta Water is a bottled water with a good hydrating ability. Better hydration may be associated with a number of benefits, including increased energy, a stronger constitution and overall improved health. I have found Penta Water to be especially beneficial for my patients with fibromyalgia, chronic fatigue, headaches and arthritis, as well as most degenerative diseases. I usually recommend two 16-ounce bottles of Penta Water a day, along with one to two quarts of filtered water.

HERE'S WHERE WE BEGIN

ARE YOU READY to start drinking two quarts of water every day?

- Your skin will look fresher.
- Your mind will function more clearly.

- It will aid in the elimination of waste.
- It will improve circulation.
- It will help to prevent numerous degenerative diseases.

Deliberately drinking water day after day will eventually become a habit. You will reach a time when you look at a soft drink, a glass of tea or cup of coffee and automatically say no. You'll ask for water instead.

Once, when my three-year-old niece, Kennedy, was visiting, I noticed how much she liked to drink sodas. So I went to the store and bought some small bottles of pure spring water. I gave her some, and surprisingly, she drank it to the last drop.

Not long after, she said, "Mommie, mommie, more water!"

My sister was amazed. "How on earth did you get her to drink that water? She's never asked for it before."

The answer is that our bodies yearn for pure, clean water—not a glass from the tap that possibly contains toxic chemicals.

Just because you've read this information, don't try to impose it on every person in your family. Begin by quietly drinking two quarts of water a day. Let those around you see the energy you have, the glow on your face, the healthy look of your skin and hair. They will likely say, "Whatever you're doing, I want to try it, too!"

Water! It's the basic element of your good health.

DR. COLBERT'S CHECKLIST
FOR WATER

⋏ Our bodies require approximately three quarts of water every day. (Our bodies usually receive one quart from the foods we eat, and we must drink two quarts.)

⋏ Caffeine is a diuretic and can cause you to lose water.

⋏ Water dehydration contributes to dozens of maladies—from hemorrhoids to arthritis.

⋏ Water delivers nutrients to your cells.

⋏ Drink water before and after your meals (drink only small amounts with your meals).

⋏ Space your two-quart water intake throughout the day.

⋏ Hot tap water leaches metals from your pipes.

⋏ Use a shower filter to keep chlorinated water from causing brittle hair and dry skin.

⋏ Adults should filter out fluoride.

⋏ "Solid block" filters are the best carbon filters.

⋏ Reverse-osmosis filters with activated carbon filtration are perhaps the best available.

⋏ Home water distillers are good for individuals prone to kidney stones.

3

THE DESPERATE
NEED TO DETOXIFY

A FEW WEEKS AGO I turned onto the wrong road as I was driving in a strange city. As I rounded a corner, I drove past an enormous junkyard. It seemed that the vast accumulation of broken, dirty and discarded bikes, tires, bottles and tin cans stretched out for blocks. I couldn't help but wondering, *On a different level—perhaps even on a cellular level—do our bodies look like this junkyard?* Do many of us have so many toxins, stored waste, accumulated fat and poison that our cells have become a molecular junkyard?

What you don't know about detoxification may be killing you. We are living in the most polluted times in the history of this world.

- Much of our air is contaminated.
- Most of our water is tainted.
- Our food usually contains toxins.

The tragic news is that these pollutants are entering our bodies and invading our circulation. Where is their final destination? They accumulate in our tissues and organs.

You may shrug your shoulders and say, "Well, big deal. What's wrong with a few impurities?"

Take a closer look. The toxins—especially pesticides—take up residence in our fatty tissues. Few people realize that their brains contain significant amounts of a form of fat called *phospholipids*. Our nerve cells are encased in a membrane consisting of *phospholipids*. Many toxins are fat-soluble and thus can accumulate in fatty tissues and in cell membranes, including our brains.

What is the result of a continual buildup of toxins? The symptoms and signs of toxic overload include fatigue, lack of energy, headaches, allergies and sensitivities, excessive mucus production, sinus problems, bronchitis and even pneumonia. Other symptoms include acne, forgetfulness, foggy thinking, food allergies, mood changes, gray, saggy skin, respiratory problems, joint aches, arthritis, psoriasis and poor immune function.

If you have any of these symptoms, it is extremely important that you read this chapter carefully and follow the guidelines to overcome the toxic overload.

In this chapter, I will identify some of the main toxins so that you can better understand them and reduce or eliminate their intake. In addition, you will learn to open up your systems of detoxification.

You need to avoid the obvious toxins—alcohol, cigarettes and drugs. If you have a problem in this area, seek both professional and spiritual guidance.

How the Body Handles Toxins

OUR AMAZING BODY gets rid of unwanted toxins through the colon, through our respiratory system, via perspiration, through the urinary tract, through the lymphatics and through the liver.

Here's how these systems are working on your behalf.

THE COLON

The primary method our body uses for eliminating toxins is through the colon. After being ingested and absorbed, the toxins first circulate in the blood, then go to the liver where they're detoxified. The waste products are dumped into the bile, then into the small intestines, then into the large intestines and finally excreted.

It's vital that our colon is functioning properly. For many, however, that's not the case. The United States has been called "the most constipated country on Planet Earth."

John Harvey Kellogg, a noted physician and surgeon who lived a century ago in Michigan, believed that 90 percent of all diseases were due to improper functioning of the colon—primarily constipation. He stated, "The lower end of the intestines is of the size that requires emptying every six hours. But by habit we retain its contents for twenty-four hours. The result is ulcers and cancer."

Dr. Kellogg lived to be ninety-one. One of the patients he was treating was C. W. Post. These two men developed many of the cereals marketed around the world—including Kellogg's Corn Flakes and Post Toasties. In the early days these cereals were filled with colon-cleansing fiber. Over time, however, processing methods have reduced the fiber content drastically.

Your colon is an amazing organ. It is like a large drainage pipe, about five feet long (your intestines are about twenty feet in length). The colon is colonized with many things: bacteria, yeast and, in some people, parasites.

Think for a moment about the plumbing that is under your kitchen sink or your toilet. If it becomes clogged by hair, debris or other things, the pipe becomes blocked, and water starts backing up. If you don't take action, it will soon spill over and cause a disaster.

It's similar with our colon. If we become constipated, over time the waste in the colon is going to start putrefying, rotting and producing gas and toxins that will be absorbed into the blood. I have treated patients with severe body odor. The cause was usually toxins being excreted through the skin because the colon was clogged.

There are over four hundred different species of bacteria in the colon—some good and some bad. The good bacteria include Lactobacillis acidophilus and bifidus. These are the bacteria that help to neutralize cancer-causing compounds. They can also neutralize pathogenic bacteria, the bad bacteria in your colon that may synthesize carcinogenic compounds.

One of my patients was a missionary headed for India with a team. I suggested that he begin taking Lactobacillis acidophilus and bifidus—"friendly" bacteria—daily. Everyone in his group became sick with dysentery, yet because he was taking the friendly bacteria, he was able to drink the local water and didn't become ill. Why? The good bacteria neutralized the bad—it couldn't get a foothold.

So how do you get the good bacteria? You can take a capsule or powder that contains these good bacteria two to three times a day, or you can eat yogurt.

Most mornings I eat a container of yogurt containing the good bacteria. Don't choose frozen yogurt or the type that has the sugar-coated fruit at the bottom. Buy plain yogurt and add fresh, unsweetened fruit to it.

YOUR RESPIRATORY SYSTEM

Another way our body clears toxins is through our respiratory system—by creating mucus. For example, when a person has a "runny nose" or is coughing mucus from the back of his throat, he is usually excreting toxins. Yet, it may also be an upper respiratory infection or an allergy.

Your lungs are usually exposed to environmental toxins more than any other organ. From cigarette smoke to exhaust that you inhale from the car in front of you at a stop light, you are being exposed to fumes, smoke and other airborne toxins every day. Goblet cells line the respiratory tract and secrete mucus that traps toxins. Other cells along the respiratory tract contain cilia, which are hairlike projections that beat about a thousand times a minute. This helps to remove particles and toxins from the lungs. Smoking tends to paralyze these cilia, making it difficult to expel the mucus and causing the characteristic "smoker's cough." Some people do not produce enough mucus, possibly due to inadequate water intake, and thus are more prone to infections. The lungs also have antioxidant enzymes such as superoxide dismutase, glutathione and catalase, which quench free radicals.

PERSPIRATION

The body also excretes toxins through the skin via perspiration.

Earlier I told you that I once stopped perspiring. During that period I developed psoriasis, and I constantly had a rash on my elbows and knees. The itching I felt was terrible, and it did not fully subside until my body was detoxified. Today, the psoriasis is kept under control through diet and detoxification. If I eat the wrong foods, however, the problem can recur.

It's important to sweat. Centuries ago the Finnish people began using saunas in the winter to help them detoxify. Because it was so cold in Finland, they couldn't get out and exercise, so they headed for a sauna. Perhaps they didn't know it, but they were excreting toxins from their bodies.

You may want to try this Finnish custom of using a sauna. The temperature of the sauna should be between 130 to 160 degrees, and you should stay in it for at least fifteen minutes. Take with you a thermos of water so you won't get dehydrated. Your goal is not to lose weight, but to shed toxins. One word of warning: *People who have heart problems or a serious medical illness should consult their physician before using a sauna.* An infrared sauna is even more effective in removing toxins, and the temperature is kept lower, usually only 100–150 degrees, which is more comfortable. I have one at home and in my office,which my patients, as well as myself, use regularly to detoxify the body through perspiration.

Recently, my wife and I escaped to a resort hotel in South Florida for a quick weekend getaway. Just after we checked in, Mary headed to the gym for a workout.

"What did you do to your skin?" I asked when she returned. "Did you get some kind of a makeover or facial?"

"No," she told me. "I spent twenty minutes on the Stairmaster, then hit the steam room and sauna. I've really been sweating!"

It made an immediate, noticeable difference in the radiance, glow, color and tone of her skin.

Aerobic exercise is highly beneficial, but be sure to perspire. When you are finished exercising or taking a sauna, don't allow the poisons to go back into your system. Take a shower and wash them off.

Infrared saunas such as the TheraSauna use an infrared radiant heat source similar to those used by doctors and physical therapists. This superior method of detoxification allows your body to secrete up to three times more perspiration than that of conventional saunas. Not only does this natural process rid your body of harmful toxins, but also it may ultimately burn up to 300 calories during a twenty- to thirty-minute session.

The infrared sauna stimulates the cellular metabolism and breaks up the water molecules that hold toxins within the body, thus allowing the body to void these toxins through perspiration. These treatments combined with a customized diet and nutritional program have vastly improved, restored and rejuvenated many of my patients at the cellular level, allowing them to feel better and lead a healthier lifestyle.

THE KIDNEYS

The kidneys help to eliminate toxins and foreign chemicals from the body. The kidneys have a higher blood flow than even the brain, heart or liver. They receive 25 percent of the body's total blood volume, thus causing them to have a high exposure to chemicals and toxins in the blood. They redistribute and reabsorb 99 percent of the blood volume, and only 0.1 percent of the filtered blood becomes urine. The best way to detoxify the kidneys is to drink adequate water, at least two quarts of water, daily.

THE LIVER

The liver is the main organ of detoxification. The liver synthesizes and secretes approximately one quart of bile, which carries toxins out through the liver to the intestines where they are excreted as waste. As the toxins enter the liver, there are two phases of detoxification that take place in the liver.

During the first phase, enzymes present in the liver begin to break down the chemical bonds in the toxins and make them water-soluble in preparation for the second phase.

Nutrients that are very important to the phase 1 process include:

- Choline (found in oatmeal, cabbage, cauliflower and soybeans)

- Milk thistle (200 milligrams three times a day)
- Lecithin (granular, 1 tablespoon one to two times daily)
- Good fats (fish oil, flaxseed oil, extra-virgin olive oil)
- Vitamins and minerals (I recommend a comprehensive multivitamin/mineral supplement such as Divine Health Multivitamins.)

Some of the toxins contained in the liver become even more chemically active and toxic during this phase. Therefore, it is very important that the body carefully synchronize these two phases. If phase 1 is faster than phase 2, a toxic overload of chemical intermediates can occur to the liver, damaging the cells.

During phase 2 the liver attaches enzymes to the chemically active intermediates through a process called *conjugation*. The enzymes work to flush out the chemical intermediates and continue to break them down so they can eventually be eliminated through the colon. The liver needs plenty of enzymes available to complete this phase.

Nutrients that are very important to help the phase 2 process include the amino acids glycine, cysteine, N-acetyl cysteine, taurine, L-glutathione and D-glucarate. Garlic is also very beneficial. B vitamins and the minerals magnesium, manganese, selenium, sulfur, zinc and molybdenum are also very important. You can find these vitamins and minerals in a comprehensive multivitamin; however, you may need to take specific amino acid supplements such as N-acetyl cysteine, taurine and glycine to help supply the raw materials for conjugation. Of these amino acids, glutathione is most important. It is the most important—and most abundant—antioxidant in our body. It can be obtained from the following supplements:

- N-acetyl cysteine (500 milligrams two to three times a day)
- Reduced L-glutathione (500 milligrams, one to two tablets, two to three times a day)

- Many vegetables (including broccoli, broccoli sprouts, cauliflower and other cruciferous vegetables and spinach)
- Whey protein (one to two scoops daily)

SOURCES OF HAZARDOUS TOXINS

IN MY EXPERIENCE as a physician I've seen symptoms triggered by dozens of causes, but there are certain sources of toxins that are major culprits. Here are some toxins—not in any order of importance—that need to be significantly reduced in your diet.

1. CAFFEINE

I remember the afternoon my wife, Mary, complained, "I don't know what's the matter with me, but I have this horrible headache. Maybe you should check me out."

My answer surprised her. "I know what's wrong," I smiled. "You forgot to drink your cup of coffee this morning." Then I added, "I want you to drink just one cup and watch what happens."

A few hours later, I asked, "What happened to your headache?"

"I don't know. It's gone!" she replied with amazement.

Caffeine is like a drug. If you don't have it on a daily basis, you can experience withdrawal. And Mary's withdrawal symptom was her headache.

It is best to decrease drastically the amount of caffeine consumed. Many people have to be weaned off caffeine slowly because they are so addicted. If they stop "cold turkey," they may experience withdrawal symptoms, including headaches.

One of my patients, a man who was drinking three pots of coffee daily, suffered from extreme exhaustion. To treat his lack of energy he was taking another toxin (coffee), which was adding to his fatigue.

One of the dangers of caffeine is that it overstimulates and may eventually weaken your adrenal glands—two small glands that sit above your kidneys. They are important because they control your "fight-or-flight" response—your ability to handle stress. Over time, your adrenal glands may become exhausted, and you may then suffer from chronic fatigue.

Caffeine can also interfere with the proper absorption of vitamins and minerals. That is why I don't recommend taking vitamins with coffee.

Another danger of caffeine is that it can increase heart rate and, in some people, cause an arrhythmia—an irregular rapid heartbeat.

Coffee imported from some countries is loaded with pesticides in larger amounts than the U.S. government allows. Pesticides are added to prevent bugs from eating the coffee beans in shipment. We say, "Oh, that is delicious," as we swallow these pesticides.

If you must have coffee, it's best to buy a product that is organically grown and to limit the consumption to one-half to one cup daily.

2. FATS IN MEAT AND DAIRY PRODUCTS

On a drive through the countryside we often see grazing cattle. Few people realize, however, that these animals are grazing on land that has usually been sprayed with pesticides. The toxins in that spray are absorbed into the blood of the cattle and deposited in their fatty tissues.

I warn people constantly about the risks of eating fatty cuts of red meat since the fat may contain high concentrations of pesticides and may also contain antibiotics, sulfa drugs, hormones and other toxins. What is the danger? Those same toxins in meat may become toxins in your fatty tissues, including your brain, prostate and breasts.

Here's my advice: Either switch to a leaner cut of meat (such as a lean fillet) or eat "free-range" meats from cattle grazed on lands not sprayed with pesticides.

Do your best to avoid consuming "organ meats"—liver and

kidney. "Wait a minute, Dr. Colbert," one woman said to me. "I love liver. That's where I get my iron."

"Well, you'll also be eating highly concentrated toxins," I responded.

The liver is a detoxing organ that acts like a trap or filter. Why transfer these dangerous chemicals into *your* body? There are much better sources of iron.

Avoid cold cuts or any packaged meats such as bologna, salami and processed ham or turkey. You may say, "I thought turkey was good for you." Breast of chicken or turkey is excellent, but it's best to stay away from cured, processed meats because of the high amounts of nitrates they contain. They may form *nitrosamines*, a fancy name for a cancer-causing chemical.

Limit, or totally avoid, pork products. Studies have shown it contains more toxins than most other meats. Perhaps that is why Scripture warned us thousands of years ago that we should not eat pork. The Lord said to Moses, "Pig may not be eaten" (Lev. 11:7). Once, Jesus cast out demons and sent them into swine—and they ran off the cliff (Matt. 8:30–32). Good riddance!

Pork is not only high in toxins, but many times it is also infected with bacteria and parasites. And those parasites are passed on to us. You may think that this is not a problem in America. Wrong! As many as one out of two people you meet could be harboring parasites.

3. TRANS FATS

Ten years ago medical experts were preaching, "Avoid eating butter. Switch to margarine—it's lower in fat."

Now, those same experts are warning, "Don't eat margarine. The trans fats it contains are not good for you."

What are trans fats? They are hydrogenated (or partially hydrogenated) fats. Hydrogenation is a process that makes an unsaturated fat more saturated. We find hydrogenated fats in margarine, shortening, fried foods, most breads and baked goods, snack foods, many prepackaged foods, chocolate and candy. They have been found to be as harmful, and possibly more harmful, to your arteries as saturated fat, and they are implicated in heart disease and cancer.

To determine whether you are eating these dangerous fats, read the nutritional labels on the food you buy. Trans fats can be found on a nutritional label under the name "hydrogenated" or "partially hydrogenated" soybean oil (or any other type of oil or shortening). These deadly oils are found in nearly all margarines, breads and baked goods, as well as in many other processed foods found in most supermarkets.

Let me warn you as gently, yet as sternly, as I can—these fats are killers!

Each of us has trillions of cells, and each cell has around it a fatty layer called the cell membrane. Over time, a continued intake of trans fats will allow them to be incorporated into the membranes, causing problems with cellular metabolism and permitting toxins to enter the cells.

I'm not against fat. In fact, the average body is made up of about 20–30 percent fat—including our cell membranes and the hormones we produce—and we need fat to survive. That's why the person who says, "Avoid all fats," is wrong. There are good fats (such as flaxseed oil), and there are bad fats.

4. FOOD ADDITIVES

If you examine food labels, you will usually find a long list of additives—dyes, chemical preservatives and compounds.

Here's one example. NutraSweet, containing aspartame, is said to be two hundred times sweeter than sugar. But it also could be two hundred times more toxic.

NutraSweet is made up of methanol and the amino acids phenylalanine and aspartic acid. What is methanol? *Webster's Dictionary* defines it as "a light volatile, flammable, poisonous liquid alcohol." Methanol is converted to formaldehyde—better known as embalming fluid. Is that what you want to be taking into your body?

Please don't think I'm on a one-man crusade against NutraSweet. These facts are widely held by informed medical authorities and nutritionists.

A common sign of methanol excess or toxicity is a headache. I have patients in my office almost every week who complain of this ailment. When I learn of their dietary history, many are taking in two to three quarts of diet colas with NutraSweet every day.

It sounds rather simple, but I take them off their diet colas and have them drink water instead—and their headaches usually disappear. All they needed was a little detoxification advice.

The research is piling up. NutraSweet has been linked to memory loss, fatigue, dizziness, nausea, blurred vision, depression, hyperactivity in children and adults and ringing in the ears.

If you experience any of these symptoms, eliminating this food additive from your diet is one of the best decisions you can make.

5. Drugs and medicines

Patients have come to my office who are taking ten to twenty different medications. We should be aware of the effect multiple medicines have on our bodies. Medicines are broken down in the liver—the great detoxifier. A study of biochemistry will show you how this detoxification process works.

What happens when we are flooded with pharmaceutical medications? They may overwhelm our liver and may leave toxic intermediates circulating in our blood. That's why, if you are on multiple medications, it is important (with the advice of a good nutritional doctor) to switch over gradually from prescriptions to vitamins, minerals, amino acids and herbs. These are not only good for your body, but they are also rarely ever toxic to the body.

FRUITS AND VEGETABLES SOURCES FOR TOXINS

IN A DISCUSSION of healthy eating, a friend commented, "I don't have much to worry about since I eat plenty of fruits and vegetables."

Just because an item is in the fresh produce department of your grocery store doesn't mean it is good for your health. Be cautious. Much of what is on display has been sprayed with pesticides and herbicides, which will make their way to your fatty tissues.

In my book *Walking in Divine Health*, I list the foods with the highest dangers. In general, products with the thickest peel—such as oranges and grapefruit—have fewer pesticides. It's the "thin peels" such as strawberries, cherries, grapes and peaches that need to be washed thoroughly. Better yet, choose organic fruits with thin peels. Of particular concern are raisins and peanuts. Although these foods contain toxins, they are not nearly as toxic as the fat in meat.

Don't always be tempted when you see beautiful shiny apples. The wax coating is often what attracts you, and it usually contains a herbicide or pesticide. Wash the apple carefully. Water alone will not usually remove the residue; you need to use a detergent to get it off. There are some great products for cleaning fruit and vegetables available at your health food store. Or use a standard detergent, then wash thoroughly with water.

Ideally, we would always choose produce that is organically grown, but it is often too expensive. Select the foods you need, and make sure they are properly washed.

It's in the Air

EVERY SECOND OF every day we depend on oxygen—it is the very breath of life. Unfortunately, oxygen cannot be stored in the body. We must rely on outside sources.

Oxygen deprivation to the arteries leads to atherosclerosis. The lungs and cardiovascular system deliver oxygen to the trillions of cells in your body. Each of these cells depends on oxygen every second to operate at peak performance. So if you are not receiving adequate oxygen due to heart disease, lung disease, sleep apnea or inadequate exercise, you may be creating an atmosphere for cancer and heart disease.

The lungs and cardiovascular system never take a break. If they did, it would result in our certain death. That's why we have no alternative to supplying our bodies with healthy air.

To get oxygen into the cells, the red blood cells must pass through tiny microscopic blood vessels called *capillaries*. They are so small that the red blood cells must go in single file—barely making it through. As they enter, oxygen is transferred to the cell. Then the red cell grabs the waste products (including carbon dioxide) and departs.

We depend on that process happening millions of times every day. Exercise increases the oxygenation to these cells.

The air we breathe at sea level is 21 percent oxygen, 72 percent nitrogen and 7 percent other gases, which include carbon dioxide. Two-time Nobel laureate Otto Warburgh believed that a lack of oxygen at the cellular level may be the main cause of cancer. He also showed that normal cells that were in tissue culture could become cancer cells when they were deprived of oxygen. Also, oxygen could kill cancer cells in tissue culture.[1]

If you've ever been seated near a smoker in a restaurant or in a public place, you are breathing carbon monoxide. That ingredient of smoke displaces oxygen from the red blood cells and decreases the oxygen-carrying capacity of the blood.

Why should you move away from a smoker? Because you're being robbed of oxygen!

Mercury is also a problem. How does it affect the oxygen? Mercury binds to the hemoglobin molecule—decreasing the oxygen-carrying capacity of the hemoglobin. This lowered oxygen tension in our blood due to mercury may predispose a person to developing cancer or atherosclerosis. The air we breathe needs to be as toxin free as possible.

We should be concerned because dangerous chemicals are everywhere—in solvents, paints, paint thinners, stain removers, varnishes, ammonia, bleach, furniture polish and so much more.

- Formaldehyde is present in the particleboard that is used to make furniture. It's also in carpet padding, carpet, upholstered furniture, curtains, bedding, pillows and many personal care products.
- Ozone is emitted from kitchen appliances.
- Pesticide residues occur from exterminators.

I remember many years ago our home was being sprayed by an extermination company. "If you have parakeets, take them outside," the worker said.

I thought, *If this can kill a parakeet, what will it do to me?*

I spoke with a veterinarian who is convinced that the potent pesticides used in homes is the reason he is seeing at least one to two cancers in animals every day.

Don't allow auto vapors from your garage to seep into your house. Carbon monoxide can kill.

Do you realize that the epoxy adhesives on electronic equipment (such as computers, microwaves and television sets) release gases when heated? Many cleaning products release toxic vapors, such as ammonia and chlorine, which irritate your lungs and eyes.

Remember, what is in the air ends up in your blood and eventually reaches every cell in your body.

A patient who works in an old downtown building told me, "I don't know why, but every time I walk into that building I get sick!" A teacher shared a similar story about her school. It's part of the "sick-building syndrome"—and the outgasing of chemicals from materials used in the construction and maintenance of those structures.

What steps can you take to address the problem? How do we clean the air?

- Open a door or window during the day or at night for at least a short period of time. Then turn on a fan to air out your living or work space.

- If you're worried about security and don't want to unlock your windows, invest in an air purifier. *Hepa filters* remove air particles with almost 100 percent efficiency. They are also available with a carbon filter that removes odors, smoke, gases and chemicals.

- Consider an *ionizing filter* that causes particles to be knocked out of the air by charging them and creating activated oxygen. It purifies the air and kills germs.

- Buy some indoor plants. They create oxygen in the air and can neutralize toxins and poisons in chemicals. Ferns, ivy and spider plants are good choices.

- Replace your air conditioning filters at least every six months. In some cases, you may need to replace them every month.

- Clean your heating and air-conditioning ducts at least every five years. Many ducts are filled with dust and toxic materials that can cause many health problems.

- Keep pets out of your bedroom. You don't need to breathe dog or cat fur when you're trying to rejuvenate your body.

- Avoid air fresheners that contain pesticides or are petroleum based. You can find a wide range of safe, effective brands in both mainstream supermarkets and health food stores. Fragrance jars and dried botanicals are among the safest. You can also find some safe non-aerosol pumps. Choose natural products. As an air freshener substitute, use a lemon spray or essential oils such as lavender.

- Choose cleaners with white distilled vinegar, borax, baking soda, lemon juice or peroxide. A solution of half water and half white distilled vinegar with a little lemon juice makes an excellent cleaner for counter tops, toilets and even floors. Hydrogen peroxide is an effective disinfectant.

- Choose natural pesticides.

THE DANGERS WE FACE

WHAT TOXINS IS your body struggling to eliminate? Diets high in fats, such as fatty meats, and low in fiber will predispose a person to develop cancer. Why? Because high meat intake will decrease the number of "good" bacteria in the colon and will increase the amount of "bad" bacteria such as *Clostridia*. The *Clostridia* bacteria in turn may produce an overabundance of toxic substances that promote the development of colon cancer.

Colon cancer, one of the leading causes of death, is on the rise because of the increase of harmful bacteria in the colon and constipation. Tragically, we are seeing colon cancer at younger and younger ages—even affecting people in their thirties. Again, it's linked to chronic constipation, a deficiency of good bacteria, an overabundance of harmful bacteria and inadequate intake of water and fiber. Constipation may lead to hemorrhoids or irritable bowel syndrome, and it may eventually lead to polyps and even cancer.

As you read about each of the dangers on the pages that follow, watch for the clues to help you know how to detoxify your body of these factors.

THE YEAST FACTOR

Not only do we have bacteria in the colon, but we also have *yeast* in the colon. Have you gone into a restaurant and been served those huge, fluffy yeast rolls? They are not only delicious, but for many they may also be hazardous to their health. When your bowel has too much yeast in it, your stomach imitates that roll—it can swell up and make you feel miserable. Even Alka-Selzer may not come to the rescue.

How do you reduce the yeast? Six ways:

1. **Avoid or greatly decrease your intake of sugar since yeast loves sugar.**
2. **Avoid antibiotics as much as possible. If you must take antibiotics, take a capsule or tablet of "good bacteria" that contains acidophilus and bifidus at**

least three times a day. If you are not sensitive to dairy foods, plain yogurt once or twice daily may also be effective at replacing the good bacteria.

3. Avoid cortisone.
4. Avoid alcohol.
5. Avoid or decrease as much as possible starches (bread, pasta, potatoes, corn, cereals, pretzels and popcorn) since they are converted into sugar.
6. Avoid yeast foods such as mushrooms, vinegar, mustard, pickles and yeast rolls.

Eating the above items will usually cause yeast to flourish. I also recommend taking garlic in a dose of 500 milligrams three or four times a day. I commonly prescribe the medication Nystatin. You can obtain this from a medical doctor who is nutritionally minded.

Some may say, "What's the big deal? A little yeast won't hurt anyone. So my stomach swells a little!"

Yeast may release toxins such as acetaldehyde, a type of alcohol that circulates throughout your blood and causes irritability, fatigue and foggy thinking. The toxins are the result of yeast in your system, which is actually fermenting. Toxins from yeast may also be harmful to your nerve tissue. Yeast may cause food allergies, and it may lead to a suppressed immune system. For more information on yeast, please read my book *The Bible Cure for Candida and Yeast Infections.*

PLAGUED BY PARASITES

Half of all Americans will at some time have parasites. They come in all shapes and sizes, from tiny microscopic parasites we can't even see to small pinworms we *can* see to the long tapeworms and roundworms we don't even like to think about.

I was recently waterskiing with my son, Kyle, who is an excellent "wake boarder"—jumping the wakes, doing 360s and all the tricks. He said, "Dad, why don't you try it?"

I got out there on this little wake board and tried to get up, but it didn't work. My wife was driving the boat, and it seemed as if I were drinking half the water in the lake. It was embarrassing. I tried again and again until I had blisters on my hands, and finally said, "Give me the skis!" My son still laughs about it.

About three or four days later I felt this little gurgle in my stomach. It became worse and turned into diarrhea. It would occur one day, be gone the next, then it would return. Finally, I checked myself and found I had *giardia*, a microscopic parasite that lives in the small intestines. It is common in the lakes of Central Florida.

I treated myself with herbs, and the condition cleared within two weeks.

WHAT ABOUT WORMS?

A rather refined woman, the wife of a top executive, came to my office. Quite fidgety, she said, "I don't know how to say this. I'm just so mortified."

"What seems to be the problem?" I asked.

"Well," she continued, "I was sitting on the toilet the other day . . . and when I finished, I looked down and saw these real long worms. I just don't know what to do!"

I asked, "Well, did you bring in the specimen? Do you have it with you?"

"No," she answered. "I flushed the toilet as fast as I could!"

The next day she brought me a specimen, and we discovered that the woman had roundworms. We were able to treat her successfully with herbs, and the problem cleared up.

Yes, there are prescription medicines available, but I'm finding that herbs usually are as effective. Artemesia (wormwood), black walnut and garlic are very effective.

How can you know if you have a worm or a parasite? Start with the symptoms:

- Constipation—results from many causes and on occasion may be due to worm infestation
- Chronic diarrhea—may be due to microscopic parasites such as amoeba and giardia
- Gas and bloating—could be not only from yeast, but from worms or parasites
- Spastic colon—from food allergies or sensitivities, yeast overgrowth, bacterial overgrowth, inadequate good bacteria or parasites, or a combination of the above. It is commonly associated with inadequate water and fiber intake.

If you are experiencing any of these symptoms, ask your doctor to perform the appropriate tests such as stool cultures, stool for ova and parasites on three separate occasions or a comprehensive digestive stool analysis with parasitology from the Great Smokies Diagnostic Labs.

MORE ABOUT MERCURY

We have discussed the menace of mercury previously, yet its threat cannot be overemphasized. Mercury has been around for thousands of years and is usually the major toxic mineral in our system. They once treated syphilis with mercury—until they found that more people were dying from the cure than from the condition.

We know that mercury, as an industrial waste, pollutes many of our waters and contaminates our fish—especially in the waters around many large factories. This toxic mineral is found in tuna, swordfish, shark and a growing list of both ocean and freshwater fish. Mercury has even been found in "farmed" fish because of the polluted water.

Mercury is an extremely toxic mineral that can weaken your immune system, trigger degenerative diseases and shorten your life. How? It competes with minerals such as magnesium, selenium, zinc and potassium for the same binding sites. Even more perilous, it can nudge out minerals that are essential for life.

Here's another problem. Mercury forms an insoluble complex with selenium, so that selenium cannot serve as the cofactor for glutathione peroxidase, which helps prevent oxidation and degeneration of our cells. (Glutathione peroxidase is the most important antioxidant that is manufactured in the body.) This selenium-based super antioxidant protects us from disease. It is stronger than either vitamin E or vitamin C. But with the interaction of mercury with selenium, glutathione peroxidase becomes ineffective in our system. That's why it is so critically important to identify and eliminate mercury from our bodies.

To the person who has chronic fatigue, fibromyalgia, arthritis or degenerative diseases and also has a mouthful of silver fillings, I recommend that you make an appointment with a good biological dentist who is experienced in the proper protocol for mercury removal.

Mercury can also be detected through an analysis of hair, urine or feces.

ARE YOU COLLECTING CADMIUM?

Starting a century ago, a toxic mineral surfaced that has caused enlarged hearts, high blood pressure and decreased kidney function. The mineral is cadmium. Before the mining of cadmium began, it caused no problems. Then suddenly it was everywhere—in our air, in our water and in our food. One of the food sources that can give us a whopping dose of cadmium is shellfish.

Old Testament law forbids eating shellfish: "You may not, however, eat marine animals that do not have both fins and scales. You are to detest them" (Lev. 11:10).

Shellfish include lobster, crab, shrimp, oysters and clams—and God told us to avoid these creeping creatures. They have been called "cockroaches of the sea" since they gather and ingest the filth and debris of the other fish and animals that live in the ocean. These "garbage collectors" take in viruses, waste material and significant amounts of cadmium—which may result in cadmium toxicity.

Cadmium is not only found in shellfish, but in coffee, tea and refined foods such as white flour, white rice and sugar. It is also in our water supply—especially in galvanized pipes. That's one of the reasons I warn people about the dangers of drinking tap water. We need to be using water that is filtered or bottled.

Cigarette smokers should be wary of elevated amounts of cadmium. Even those who inhale secondhand smoke need to be concerned. Avoid exposure to any kind of tobacco smoke—it can poison you.

If you travel to cities where the air pollution is high, stay indoors as much as possible and invest in a small air purifier to place in your hotel room.

As we age, cadmium collects in our tissues, especially in our liver and kidneys. Since it is difficult to remove, your first objective should be prevention.

To be proactive against this toxic mineral, take plenty of zinc. Why? Cadmium occupies the zinc receptor sites in our body, so if we take more zinc, we can help prevent cadmium toxicity.

Your doctor can determine if you have excessive amounts of cadmium in your system through a hair analysis or a six-hour urine test for cadmium. If it's high, chelation can (over time) pull the cadmium out of your body and help improve kidney functions dramatically. Chelation therapy is an intravenous therapy that utilizes EDTA along with intravenous vitamins and minerals to chelate or pull out toxic metals such as lead, cadmium and aluminum.

GET THE LEAD OUT

Compared with other toxic minerals, we've known about the dangers of lead for decades. It can have a devastating effect on the brain and the nervous system.

Lead is found in almost every food, especially if it's grown near an industrialized area or close to a busy highway. Here's the cycle. Particles are carried through the air, they settle in the ground, they are picked up by plants and animals, and we ingest them in our food.

Foods such as liver, luncheon meat and sausage may have elevated levels of lead and need to be avoided. Also, we need to be concerned about the water pipes in older homes and hotels. The soldering of these pipes may have been done with lead. It's another reason to avoid tap water and to use a water filter.

The lead used in the soldering of many tins cans may be harmful. It's best to eat fresh fruit and vegetables. Examine your cooking utensils and food storage containers since lead may reside in earthenware.

Lead inactivates zinc, copper and iron—important minerals. It also acts to bind sulfur-containing enzymes.

Every time I see someone jogging or biking along a busy highway, I want to stop them and say, "Your exercise is not worth the effort!" They're inhaling hydrocarbons and other toxins from engine exhaust and also may be inhaling lead.

You can do more harm by exercising alongside a busy highway than by *not* exercising. And if you're driving a convertible in heavy traffic, close the top.

To decrease lead in your system, use the same basic toxin-removing techniques we have mentioned earlier. And be sure to take a mineral supplement with calcium and magnesium. Your supplement should include 500 milligrams of calcium and 250 milligrams of magnesium. Take the supplement two times a day. For serious conditions, chelation therapy can pull out the lead. (See page 200.)

AVOID ALUMINUM

Approximately 14 percent of the earth's crust is composed of aluminum, and the average person ingests 30 to 50 milligrams of this toxic mineral every day. More and more research into the devastating disease of Alzheimer's continues, and more and more doctors believe that aluminum plays a critical role. For example, when autopsies are performed on Alzheimer's patients, there are accumulations in the brain called *neurofibrillary tangles*—which are simply collections of aluminum. Whether Alzheimer's disease is caused by aluminum or whether aluminum is merely attracted into the neurofibrillary tangles in the brain is still being argued in medical circles.

Here are just a few products we use every day that contain aluminum:

- *Antacids.* In addition to being dangerous to your digestive system, many popular antacids—including Mylanta, Rolaids, Maalox Plus and Riopan—contain aluminum. Examine the labels.
- *Household baking powders.* Most of these products contain about 6 percent aluminum. Self-rising flours have approximately 6.5 percent.
- *Nondairy creamers.* They contain as much as 16 percent aluminum.
- *Processed cheese.* Most have about 3.5 percent aluminum.
- *Table salt.* So that it doesn't cake, significant amounts of aluminum are found in salt.

- *Aluminum cookware and aluminum foil.* The residue from these products can be transferred to our bodies.
- *Aluminum cans.* Aluminum, which is neurotoxic, leaches into the drinks contained in aluminum containers. Use glass containers as much as possible.
- *Antiperspirants.* The aluminum in your antiperspirant is a key ingredient that stops you from sweating. Immediately switch to a deodorant—and even then look at the label to be sure there is no aluminum. Remember, sweating is important to detoxification.

We simply cannot avoid ingesting some aluminum from the foods we eat. Our goal should be to avoid it wherever possible.

Body odor

Several years ago a friend of mine had a severe case of body odor. You could smell him from across the room. He sadly confided, "I can take a shower, scrub myself and put on deodorant; yet in a few minutes the odor will come back."

The armpits of his shirts became yellow, and both he and his wife were very concerned. At that time in my medical experience I didn't have an answer.

Then one day a patient came to my office with the exact same problem. I immediately reflected on what I had learned at recent seminars and through study, and asked, "How often do you have a bowel movement?"

"Well, about every three days," he answered.

We put him on a good water, fiber and colon detox program, and within one week the odor was gone.

Free radicals

Our bodies are constantly producing toxins. When we are stressed out, what do we produce? *Excessive free radicals.* They are simply unpaired electrons moving through our body attempting to "pair up." In the process, they damage our cells.

Our bodies also produce excessive free radicals when we're around noxious stimuli such as cigarette smoke, smog, car exhaust or industrial pollution. They also result from eating toxic foods.

The best way to address the problem is to take an antioxidant—available at any health food store. In the following section, I will discuss the use of antioxidants for detoxification. By using these antioxidants, you can prevent free-radical damage.

WHAT IS DETOXIFICATION?

MOST PHYSICIANS SEE a problem and prescribe a pill. In this case, however, the symptom may not indicate the root cause. For example, if a person has drainage from the nose, is the solution a capsule to dry the passageway? That may be a temporary solution, but the drainage may be caused by an accumulation of toxins—creating a need for the individual to detoxify. If prescribed, medicine may actually add to the toxic burden.

Detoxification is simply reducing or removing our toxin intake and improving the six main elimination systems of our body:

1. Our kidneys—which filter the blood and excrete waste products
2. Our colon—the sewage system of our body
3. Our lungs—which have the greatest exposure to the environment
4. Our liver—which transforms chemicals and toxins in order to remove them from the body
5. Our skin
6. Our lymphatics (see page 205)

I wish I could tell you that every toxin that enters your body can be eliminated. Living on our polluted planet, however, makes that impossible.

YOUR PLAN FOR DETOXIFICATION

WHEN THERE IS an excess of any toxin intake or an excess of toxin production—or if you are not eliminating toxins—you are eventually going to have a problem with toxicity, which usually leads to disease. The symptoms will start occurring.

Don't despair. If your body has good elimination functions you can handle most toxins. You don't need to move to another location or check into a hospital. You can "detox" right where you are. Here are the essentials:

1. *Water.* Read chapter two and follow the recommendations.
2. *Bowel regularity.* Adhere to a high-fiber diet—not one that is filled with fats, processed white sugar, white flour and full of meats. According to the American Cancer Society, you need 30 grams of fiber every day. I believe this will help to prevent colon cancer and other colon problems.

Remember, a bowel movement occurs about eighteen to twenty-four hours after a meal. Your regularity is timed to the meals you had one or two days earlier. More than one bowel movement a day is ideal; however, one bowel movement a day is satisfactory. But one bowel movement every three days or once a week spells toxicity overload.

I know that changing your diet is difficult, yet it is essential. Start by eating a high-fiber cereal, high-fiber vegetables such as beans, peas, lentils and whole grains. Include pears and apples.

I recommend a fiber supplement you can find at any drug store, health food store, Wal-Mart or K-Mart. Fiber supplements are quite inexpensive. You can even take a teaspoon of psyllium with 8 ounces of water when you get out of bed every morning. It's great for regularity. Repeat the process at night. Start slowly, because fiber may produce excessive gas and bloating. If you want something easier on your system, go to a health food store and buy some rice bran fiber.

Daily exercise is also important for regularity. You don't need to go the gym, run, cycle, swim or lift weights. Walking briskly is extremely effective. It helps to stimulate peristalsis (contraction) of the colon.

Vitamin C is also vital for bowel regularity. I recommend Divine Health Buffered Vitamin C, one capsule two to three times a day. It is best not to take vitamin C with the fiber, since the fiber may bind the mineral ascorbates. Because buffered vitamin C contains magnesium, it will help to regulate your bowels. To avoid possible diarrhea, start with one tablet a day.

Magnesium is a wonderful mineral that helps to regulate the colon and bowels. If you have ongoing problems with constipation (going every two or three days), I recommend a magnesium supplement such as magnesium citrate. Magnesium citrate, taken in a dose of 400 milligrams, one to two capsules, three times a day will usually regulate the bowel movement. Magnesium citrate may also be taken as a liquid.

If you still have problems, consult your physician. You may need an examination of the colon such as a sigmoid exam, a colonoscopy or a barium enema.

Herbs and nutrients

To detoxify your body, I recommend several herbs and nutrients that are high in chlorophyll, including wheatgrass, barley grass, alfalfa, spirulina, chlorella and blue-green algae. These high-chlorophyll foods are excellent colon cleansers and detoxifiers.

Every morning I take a little scoop (about a heaping tablespoon) of a mixture of alfalfa, wheatgrass, barley grass, spirulina, chlorella and blue-green algae. The drink is called *Green Superfood,* and it is an excellent detoxifier and colon cleanser.

In my opinion, the best way to detox heavy metals is chlorella, which is a form of algae. There are three main algaes—spirulina, chlorella (which is high in chlorophyll) and blue-green algae. What's so beneficial about chlorella is that it has a cracked shell and is able to absorb and detoxify mercury and other heavy metals.

I am a great believer in garlic since I've seen its results. Garlic is a wonderful, natural antibiotic. It also has antiviral, antifungal, antiyeast and antiparasitic properties. Take 500 milligrams of garlic three times a day for three months if you have a yeast infection. Take it three times a day for a month or two for parasites. Take it two to three times a day for heavy metal detoxifying and to prevent viral infection.

Other effective herbs include barberry, burdock, cayenne pepper, dandelion root, echinacea, fenugreek, red clover, goldenseal, milk thistle and mullein leaf. You can also find a special colon and body detox program that contains these detoxifying herbs at health food stores.

Flaxseed oil

One of the most beneficial—and overlooked—toxin fighters is flaxseed oil. As bad as hydrogenated fats (margarine) are for your body, flaxseed oil is *good* for you. It helps the body overcome the effects of pesticides and industrial toxins and is one of the most important detoxing tools available. I believe everyone should take 1 tablespoon of flaxseed oil once or twice a day—I certainly do. It's very rich in omega-3 fatty acids and strengthens your cell membranes. It also may help to prevent heart disease, arthritis and even cancer. Flaxseed oil is a type of "fat exchange" program. You are actually exchanging the bad fats for good fats. That is why it's so critically important.

If you don't like the taste, try cinnamon flaxseed oil.

THE BENEFITS OF FASTING

One of the greatest methods of detoxing is fasting. In the Bible, Jesus said, "When you fast...," not "If you fast..." (Matt. 6:16). The Bible *expects* us to fast—whether it is for one day a week or one day a month.

I am a great believer in fasting, not only for its undisputed spiritual benefits, but also for the cleansing of the body that accompanies it. For medical reasons, I do not recommend a fast for over seven days. I insist that my patients drink at least two to three quarts of water a day. Remember, you can live for five or so weeks without food, but only five days without water.

When animals become sick they fast. For you and me, fasting will help prevent colds, flus, allergies, high blood pressure, asthma, headaches, psoriasis, heart disease, arthritis, back pain and fatigue.

Although the Bible tells us that Jesus fasted for forty days, I would never tell anyone to go on a forty-day fast. Why? If you're not *called by God* to go without food for such a long period, there could be dangerous consequences.

I've seen many patients who fast too long—and too often. Some say, "I feel so good I'm going to fast five, six or seven days a month." Suddenly, they begin losing muscle mass, their immune system is affected, and they begin to get sick.

Fasting should be for very brief periods of time, not longer than three to seven days unless closely monitored by your doctor. You should not do it if you are about to have surgery (or recently had an operation), have ulcer disease, any mental illness, cancer, heart disease, arrhythmias, heart failure, weakened immune system or if you are underweight. Fasting too often leads to malnourishment, fatigue, weakness from lack of nutrition and a lower resistance to disease. Women who are pregnant or lactating should not be fasting.

I recommend that people fast on a "rest" day rather than a work day, lest your mind become cloudy and your job performance suffer. I also feel that a juice fast (with fresh-squeezed juices) is much safer than a water fast. It's essential to drink two quarts of pure water a day during the fast—remember, we're flushing out our bodies. Take your flaxseed oil, 1 teaspoon with 8 ounces of juice, which will help with hunger.

This type of fast is safer, easily assimilated, stimulates removal of waste, supplies many of the nutrients we need and prevents excessive muscle loss.

For variations on the theme:

- Add 1 tablespoon freshly squeezed lemon juice to 8 ounces of water. You may add Stevia (an herbal sweetener).
- Try a carrot-juice fast—with fresh juice every three to four hours. Add 1 teaspoon of flaxseed oil to 8 ounces to prevent hunger.
- For a super cleanse, create a drink of 2 tablespoons of fresh-squeezed lemon juice with just $\frac{1}{10}$ teaspoon of cayenne pepper. Mix with 8 ounces of water. Drink every three to four hours.
- Add 1 tablespoon of your favorite chlorophyll food such as Green Superfood to your favorite juice and repeat three to four times a day. This is my favorite fasting method. In addition, you should drink two quarts of water a day.

- Add 1 teaspoon of apple cider vinegar to an 8-ounce glass of water and drink every three to four hours. You can add 1 teaspoon of flaxseed oil to each of these drinks. You may try different fruit drinks during the fast for variety.

The key is to find the program that fits you best. Fast one day a week, or one day a month, to detoxify your body. If you are going to fast longer than one day, I recommend that you follow the recommendations in my book *Toxic Relief*.

A woman recently came to my office who had been to an allergist for a long series of tests. For several months she had experienced a condition called allergic urticaria. Her whole body was covered in hives, and she was miserable. She was on extremely high doses of cortisone and was taking four different antihistamines. "I feel absolutely miserable," she exclaimed.

I said, "We need to put you on a detox program that includes fasting."

In a short time she was off her cortisone and taking only a low dose of antihistamine. She was a transformed person.

Like a flowing river, God created your body both to receive and to give. What it takes in must be eliminated. Take the time to detoxify—your life may depend on it!

DR. COLBERT'S CHECKLIST
FOR DETOXIFICATION

⋏ Toxins usually reside in our fatty tissues and must be eliminated.

⋏ We must improve the main detoxification systems of our body: our kidneys, colon, skin, lungs, lymphatics and liver.

⋏ Avoid the toxins of alcohol, tobacco and drugs.

⋏ Eliminate or decrease caffeine from your diet.

⋏ Avoid liver and kidney meats because they are toxic filters in animals.

⋏ Limit, or totally avoid, pork products.

⋏ Eat seafood (but not shellfish) from nonindustrialized areas only.

⋏ Avoid trans fats, which are harmful to your arteries.

⋏ Don't eat foods high in mercury.

⋏ Engage in aerobic exercise for perspiration, and use a sauna regularly.

⋏ Decrease your intake of sugar and salt.

⋏ Eat a high-fiber diet for bowel regularity, or take a fiber supplement like psyllium.

⋏ Take 1 tablespoon of flaxseed oil, once or twice a day.

⋏ Fast at least one day each month.

4

THE DISASTER
OF DEADLY EMOTIONS

Ler me share a dynamic fact that can totally transform your life and health. How you feel in your heart can show up in your body, for your heart and body are more powerfully connected than you have ever realized.

It's true. Your emotional health is often mirrored in your physical health. Perhaps you've asked your doctor to treat your pain when you would have been better off dealing with the root problem—your deadly emotions.

When I walk into a room where a patient is waiting, I often know more about what is causing that person's problems than what is revealed on the charts. The patient's attitude speaks volumes.

I have often thought, *If a negative person can sap my energy, what must that attitude be doing to his or her own body?*

One patient who had an extremely negative outlook on life returned to my office about every two weeks. I became convinced that her constant health problems were being caused by her attitude. Her emotions were blocking her healing.

THE SPIRITUAL SIDE OF NEGATIVE EMOTIONS

NEGATIVE ATTITUDES ARE ongoing patterns of thought that begin with just one thought. Webster's dictionary defines attitude as "a manner of acting, feeling or thinking that shows one's disposition." Attitude is actually an outward feeling expressed by behavior. Your attitude shows without your saying a single word.

Bad attitudes develop from negative thoughts and negative words. Often they develop in the following ways:

- Being critical leads to envy and jealousy.
- Grumbling and murmuring lead to bitterness and resentment.
- Chronic complaining leads to selfishness and greed.
- Arrogance leads to envy and jealousy, which lead to hatred.
- Being argumentative leads to anger.
- Always seeing the negative leads to being programmed for failure, which leads to depression and hopelessness.
- Having a chip on your shoulder leads to resentment.
- Taking offense also leads to resentment.

THE PATH TO DEADLY EMOTIONS

ONCE BAD ATTITUDES have developed, the next step is the formation of deadly emotions. Deadly emotions include:

- Unforgiveness
- Bitterness
- Resentment
- Anger
- Hatred
- Abandonment

- Fear
- Shame
- Guilt
- Envy
- Jealousy
- Humiliation

Deadly emotions wreak havoc on our physical bodies. I would consider bitterness, resentment and unforgiveness to be three of the most deadly emotions a person can have. These emotions may actually prevent the body from releasing toxic material, especially from the liver and gallbladder. This buildup of toxins in the system can eventually lead to disease.

Before I treat a person with cancer, I encourage that person to release any anger, bitterness or resentment that may be harbored inside through the power of forgiveness. I will discuss how to release these emotions later in this chapter. I have found that my patients are often unable to receive their healing until they release these deadly emotions.

THE IMPACT OF DEADLY EMOTIONS

DEADLY EMOTIONS CAN also lead to deadly behaviors that affect the lives of the people around us. Deadly emotions always start in the mind with a thought. That thought leads to a word, and the word leads to an attitude. In turn, these bad attitudes lead to deadly emotions that become trapped in our bodies and set disease in motion.

HATRED AND JEALOUSY

Hatred and jealousy can lead to:

- High blood pressure
- Migraine headaches
- Heart disease
- Ulcers
- Cancer

When an individual experiences excessive anger, worry and the stress caused by hatred, his or her adrenalin level rises, blood pressure may increase, and a heavier load is placed on the heart and circulatory system. The risk of heart disease—especially heart attack—increases for those who live in attitudes of anger. These individuals experience twice the risk of heart disease as compared to everyone else.

In addition, when a person is upset, angry or fearful while eating, these negative emotions stimulate the sympathetic nervous system, which in turn causes decreased secretion of hydrochloric acid. This causes decreased secretion of pancreatic enzymes, which makes it harder to digest the food. Without adequate stomach acid and pancreatic enzymes, food is not properly digested. This may lead to bloating, gas, heartburn, indigestion and other digestive problems.

The excessive stress caused by negative emotions is quite dangerous because it increases our cortisol levels, which then suppresses the immune system. When the immune system is suppressed, cancerous cells can begin to form and grow. Hatred and jealousy are devastating emotions.

The story of Saul's bitter hatred of David is a candid illustration from the Bible. Saul, the king of Israel, hated David, who was chosen by God to replace him. As we look at the life of Saul, we can see how Saul's hatred of David began from his own negative thoughts.

Saul became acquainted with David as a result of David's heroic confrontation with Goliath. In 1 Samuel 18 we read the story of their developing relationship:

> Whatever Saul asked David to do, David did it successfully. So Saul made him a commander in his army, an appointment that was applauded by the fighting men and officers alike. But something happened when the victorious Israelite army was returning home after David had killed Goliath. Women came out from all the towns along the way to celebrate and to cheer for King Saul, and they sang and danced for joy with

tambourines and cymbals. This was their song: "Saul has killed his thousands, and David his ten thousands!"

—1 SAMUEL 18:5–7

Saul didn't like the attention the women along the parade route gave to David. No doubt he thought, *Why are they saying that David has killed his ten thousands? He's just a scrawny little kid that aimed a lucky stone at the giant. Why, everything David is today is the result of what I have done for him. Why is he getting more attention than I'm getting?*

The Bible tells us what happened next:

> This made Saul very angry. "What's this?" he said. "They credit David with ten thousands and me with only thousands. Next they'll be making him their king!" So from that time on Saul kept a jealous eye on David. The very next day, in fact, a tormenting spirit from God overwhelmed Saul, and he began to rave like a madman.
>
> —1 SAMUEL 18:8–10

Saul's negative thoughts had given him a bad attitude. His bad attitude had grown into the deadly emotions of hatred and jealousy. These deadly emotions eventually led to a state in which Saul ranted and raved like a madman. Can you imagine the door that Saul had opened for the development of high blood pressure, ulcers, migraine headaches and even cancer? His emotions flooded out of him and affected everyone around him. They clouded every decision he made, and ultimately they led to his death.

Hatred and jealousy are killers! They destroy the person first on the inside, and then they manifest in harmful actions and behaviors on the outside.

PRIDE

Pride can lead to:

- Mental illness
- Stroke
- Heart attack
- Death

One of the deadliest attitudes is pride, and it may bring about deadly consequences. The Book of Proverbs promises that submitting your heart to pride will, in fact, bring about your destruction. It says, "Pride goes before destruction, and haughtiness before a fall" (Prov. 16:18).

Pride is reported as being the deadly attitude that caused the downfall of Satan himself. The Bible says that before Satan fell into sin, he was a beautiful and very powerful angelic being. He actually thought he was greater than God.

Isaiah 14:13, 15 tells the story of the evil seed (or thought) of pride that pierced Satan's mind and heart and led to his downfall. "For you said to yourself, 'I will ascend to heaven and set my throne above God's stars. I will preside on the mountain of the gods far away in the north.' . . . But instead, you will be brought down to the place of the dead, down to its lowest depths."

Satan fell farther than any being ever fell, for he fell from heaven to hell, and it was all because of pride—that inordinate desire for superiority.

Others in the Bible followed along the same path with the same terrible results. King Herod, in Acts 12:21–23, let pride destroy him also. The Bible says:

> And an appointment with Herod was granted. When the day arrived, Herod put on his royal robes, sat on his throne, and made a speech to them. The people gave him a great ovation, shouting, "It is the voice of a god, not of a man." Instantly, an

angel of the Lord struck Herod with sickness, because he accepted the people's worship instead of giving the glory to God.

Herod's death was a result of the deadly emotion of pride. Another great king, King Nebuchadnezzar of Babylon, became mentally ill as a result of pride. Daniel 4:29–32 tells us the story:

> Twelve months later, he was taking a walk on the flat roof of the royal palace in Babylon. As he looked out across the city, he said, "Just look at this great city of Babylon! I, by my own mighty power, have built this beautiful city as my royal residence and as an expression of my royal splendor." While he was still speaking these words, a voice called down from heaven, "O King Nebuchadnezzar, this message is for you! You are no longer ruler of this kingdom. You will be driven from human society. You will live in the fields with the wild animals, and you will eat grass like a cow."

When pride overcame this mighty king's heart, insanity followed. Pride is a deadly emotion, and it's extremely subtle. Every gift and blessing in your life was given to you by God. Are you intelligent? God blessed you with a gifted mind. Are you artistic? That gift came from God as well. There is nothing that you and I have that was not given to us as a gift by our loving heavenly Father. Don't ever forget that whatever gift you've been given is from God and decide that something special about you makes you better than others. That's pride.

Stay humble, acknowledging God for the benefits of this life that He has given you by His great love. Humility and gratitude to God will protect you from the deadliest sins—the attitude of pride.

FEAR AND ANXIETY

Fear and anxiety can lead to:

- Heart disease
- Mental illness
- Panic attacks

- Depression
- Heart attack
- Phobias

Your body may respond to fear and anxiety by triggering the release of excessive amounts of adrenaline, which causes a rapid heartbeat, hyperventilation, sweaty palms and increased peristalsis (contractions) of the gastrointestinal tract. This is often referred to as your "fight-or-flight" response. In this heightened emotional state caused by fear and anxiety, many physical changes may occur that are normal. However, prolonged attitudes of fear and anxiety may cause this heightened state to be maintained too long and can actually lead to adrenal exhaustion, fatigue, anxiety and panic attacks, irritable bowel syndrome and tension headaches, in addition to other symptoms. Physical and emotional exhaustion and a weakening of your immune system can occur, and the final result can be severe illness.

Fear is a deadly emotion that paralyzes—both internally and externally. Those overcome by fear may be tormented by panic attacks, phobias and perceived dangers.

Fear and anxiety cripple our physical and emotional functioning. They hinder our relationship to God. Fear often begins with a negative thought about a frightening event or circumstance in our lives. That fear can become the focus for our feelings and actions for our entire lives unless we learn to get rid of it.

The Bible gives us an example of what I believe to be the first record of a heart attack—and it was caused by fear! During the time that David was hiding from King Saul, he heard of a wealthy man by the name of Nabal who had large herds of goats and flocks of sheep. David knew that as he warred against attacking enemies, his efforts had protected Nabal's herds. Without his intervention, Nabal would likely have lost his herds to enemy tribes.

When David heard that it was shearing time for Nabal, he sent a message to him, saying:

> Peace and prosperity to you, your family, and everything you own! I am told that you are shearing your sheep and goats. While your shepherds stayed among us near Carmel, we never harmed them, and nothing was ever stolen from them. Ask your own servants and they will tell you this is true. So would you please be kind to us, since we have come at a time of celebration? Please give us any provisions you might have on hand.
> —1 SAMUEL 25:6–8

But Nabal did not welcome David's request for provisions. He acted like he didn't even know who David was. He said, "There is no way that I'm going to take my bread, my water and my meat and give it to a man that I don't even know." Yet David's armies had been the protectors of that land, so Nabal knew very well who David was.

When David heard the response of Nabal, he became very angry. He instructed his men to go down and kill the whole household of Nabal. Because of Nabal's arrogant attitude, his whole household was about to be killed.

But Nabal was blessed with a beautiful, compassionate *and wise* wife! Abigail prepared food, sheep and all kinds of gifts for David and his men. She took these gifts to David, fell down before him and cried for mercy. Because of her humility, David granted mercy, and she was responsible for saving her whole household.

During the time that Abigail was with David, her husband, Nabal, had prepared a huge feast—a feast fit for a king. By the time Abigail arrived back home—having secured safety for her entire family—Nabal had fallen into a drunken stupor and could not be awakened.

The Bible tells us what happened the next day:

> But it came to pass in the morning, when the wine was gone out of Nabal, and his wife had told him these things, that his heart died within him, and he became as a stone.
> —1 SAMUEL 25:37, KJV

Nabal died about ten days later. Whether it was a stroke or a heart attack that killed Nabal, we cannot be sure. But the implication is clear: Fear, a deadly emotion, killed him. In Luke 21:26, Jesus was talking about the last days when He declared, "Men's hearts failing them for fear and for looking after those things which are coming on the earth" (KJV).

ANGER

Anger can lead to:

- Rheumatoid arthritis
- High blood pressure
- Heart failure
- Heart attack
- Stroke
- Ulcer disease

Anger can be a healthy emotion if it is released in a productive manner. However, when it is harbored inside, it becomes dangerous to your health. That is why Scripture says, "Don't sin by letting anger gain control over you. Don't let the sun go down while you are still angry" (Eph. 4:26).

The apostle Paul was telling us that if we don't resolve our outrage quickly, it will eat us away inside. We'll become like a pressure cooker, with anger building up until we explode and harm those around us. Or we may explode on the inside, causing a heart attack or stroke.

Without realizing that it is happening, your anger becomes bitterness, which becomes resentment, which becomes hatred. This emotional turmoil is the breeding ground for many physical diseases.

Dr. Robert Eliot, a noted cardiologist, found that when "hot reactors" internalize their feelings, they can eventually turn into hostility and rage. When that happens, blood pressure dramatically increases. People with this response are at a much higher risk for developing heart attacks and strokes. Don't let it happen to you. Release it and ask forgiveness. Don't let the sun go down on your anger.

DEPRESSION

Depression may lead to:

- Cancer
- Heart disease

Studies have shown that men have a tendency to release their anger, but women are more likely to suppress it. When bitterness, resentment and hatred are not released, it can result in depression.

Depression affects about nineteen million Americans. Women have a 10 to 25 percent risk of major depression over a lifetime, and men have about a 5 to 12 percent risk. Depression has become a global problem. One in six people around the world will suffer from major depression at some point during their lives.

Why do some men become ill after losing a job or after retirement? Is it simply old age, or is something else at work? A loss—*any* loss—may negatively affect our emotional stability and may weaken our immune system. It opens the door for a variety of illnesses, including cancer.

It is true that cancer can strike all types of people, but one of the most common factors that researchers are discovering prior to the onset of cancers is the *lack of an emotional outlet*. Again and again, when patients are asked, "Tell me about your life two or three years prior to the onset of cancer," these folks reveal deep emotional pressures, often accompanied by a major traumatic loss or depression. Such losses, together with the resultant depression, will not trigger cancer in all cases—but it may in some. Depressed men, for example, are much more likely to get cancer than men who are not depressed.

What about women? Studies reveal that homemakers develop 54 percent more cancer than the general population—and 157 percent more than women who work outside of the home. This has led researchers to look for a chemical in the household that may be causing the tumors. But could it be something invisible? Is it possible that some homemakers feel trapped, unappreciated and helpless—thus opening the door to affliction and disease? Many homemakers love their role—and they are happy and content with their lives. But some may harbor deadly emotions that may trigger physical illness—including cancer.

No way out

Many individuals experience despair, often brought about by a sudden change in circumstances or environment. No one is immune to the change that life brings to all. But some begin to suffer both mentally and physically because they feel there is no way out.

Depression and arthritis

I have often wondered, *Why do we see much more rheumatoid arthritis occurring in women than in men?*

I began to pay close attention to the studies showing that men are usually able to express their anger, whereas women tend to hold it in and become depressed. I recalled the scripture, "A broken spirit drieth the bones" (Prov. 17:22, KJV).

Could it be that a "broken spirit" in some women is causing rheumatoid arthritis? Is it is causing the joints and bones to become inflamed and begin to degenerate?

I've been afforded the privilege of witnessing God's power to heal instantly as I've traveled around the world. On more than one occasion I have seen an individual healed of arthritis when he or she released bitterness and anger through total repentance. These people were first set free spiritually, then emotionally and then physically. When the power of the deadly emotion was broken, the illness was healed.

The person who continues to seethe over some unresolved issue is not only destroying a personal relationship and harming his or her own body, but that person is blocking communication with God. A bitter person no longer has the desire to read the Word of God or pray. When you are bitter, your outlook changes, and your happiness is gone. The price of bitterness is costly.

What should be your plan of action at the first sign of anger or bitterness? Immediately go to the person involved and deal with it—regardless of who is at fault. You will feel a wave of freedom sweep over you as you forgive—regardless of how the other person responds in turn.

Deadly emotions are just that—deadly. You have seen how such emotions can rob you of life and health. Take a minute to reflect on your own heart. Do you have deadly emotions that are difficult to conquer? Keep reading to discover some powerful keys for defeating deadly emotions once and for all.

THE MIRACLE OF A MERRY HEART

TWO OF THE greatest healing forces in the world are available to you at this very moment. They are the healing power of laughter and the restorative strength of joy. A merry heart is your greatest weapon against deadly emotions.

The Bible affirms the healing power of joy when it says, "A cheerful heart is good medicine, but a broken spirit saps a person's strength" (Prov. 17:22). This scriptural truth suggests that laughter holds as much healing power as medicine. Is it any wonder that those who laugh easily often live longer than those who do not?

When you laugh, powerful chemicals called endorphins, which act much the same way as morphine, are released in the brain. Endorphins trigger a feeling of well-being throughout your entire body. So you see, a merry heart does really work like medicine!

An enormous amount of research supports this fact. If a person is happy and at peace with himself and his surroundings, he will have significantly fewer serious illnesses than the unhappy person.

In the Department of Behavioral Medicine of the UCLA Medical School, Norman Cousins conducted extensive research into the physical benefits of happiness. He established the Humor Research Task Force that coordinated worldwide clinical research on humor. The connection between stress and high blood pressure, muscle tension and the suppression of one's immune system has been understood for years. Cousin's body of research proved conclusively that laughter, happiness and joy are perfect antidotes for stress.[1]

Long ago the prophet Isaiah wrote:

> You will keep in perfect peace all who trust in you, whose thoughts are fixed on you!
>
> —Isaiah 26:3

A noted doctor once said that the diaphragm, thorax, abdomen, heart, lungs—and even the liver—are given a massage during a hearty laugh. That's a good internal workout!

Instead of watching films or television dramas that drain and depress your spirit, choose something that can put a smile on your face and feed your healthy emotions.

UNCONDITIONAL LOVE

HAVE YOU EVER felt alone and unloved? A limitless ocean of love is available to you at this very moment in time—it is no farther away than a simple prayer. Jesus Christ loves you so much that He gave His own life for you so that you could be healed, delivered from the bondage of fear and oppression, and so that you could have eternal life.

I believe deeply in the power of God. Although you cannot see it, God's power is as real today as when Jesus Christ walked the shores of Galilee. Many times I have witnessed His awesome power to touch and heal miraculously a life crippled by disease and broken by the cruelty of imminent death. But I want you to understand a secret about that wonderful power: The power of God is discovered in the power of His love. He loves you more than you could ever know! And though you may not see it, His love is reaching out to you at this very moment, seeking to fill all the places of need and hurt buried deep within you. Why don't you respond to Him right now by whispering a prayer? Tell Him, "Yes, I receive Your wonderful love for me, to heal me, to cleanse me from sin, to touch my life with renewed energy and to refresh me with spiritual joy." You'll be glad you did.

You may think, *But Dr. Colbert, you don't know what I've done.* You're right, I don't. But I do know this: Whatever you've done does not matter in the face of God's love for you. You see, His love is unconditional. You could never earn it or be worthy of it. None of us are. His love for you is great, not because of you or anything you have or haven't done. His love is great because He is

96

great. That's what God's unconditional love is all about.

Just as the lack of heartfelt love invites infirmities, I am convinced that unconditional love is the best *immune stimulator* in existence.

Once you experience the power of Christ's unconditional love, you will begin to share that same love with others, even with those who have wronged you.

Jesus was asked, "Teacher, which is the most important commandment in the law of Moses?" (Matt. 22:36). Jesus answered, "You must love the Lord your God with all your heart, all your soul, and all your mind. This is the first and greatest commandment. A second is equally important: Love your neighbor as yourself" (vv. 37–39).

To love another person as you love yourself is difficult, yet it defines unconditional love.

The Holocaust was one of the most tragic events in human history, yet in the midst of the slaughter of six million people of the Jewish race, there are stories of unparalleled love and forgiveness.

George Ritchey lived through the experience and is now a psychiatrist. In his book *Return From Tomorrow*, he relates the story of a death camp survivor who was given the nickname "Wild Bill." Ritchey writes:

> When the war in Europe ended in May 1945, the 123rd Evac entered Germany with the occupying troops. This was the most shattering experience I had yet had; I had been exposed many times by then to sudden death and injury, but to see the effect of slow starvation, to walk through these barracks where thousands of men had died a little bit at a time over a period of years, was a new kind of horror.
>
> We came to him with all sorts of problems; the paper work alone was staggering in attempting to relocate people whose families, even whole hometowns, might have disappeared.

But though Wild Bill worked fifteen and sixteen hours a day, he showed no signs of weariness. While the rest of us were drooping with fatigue, he seemed to gain strength. "We have time for this old fellow," he'd say. "He's been waiting to see us all day." His compassion for his fellow prisoners glowed on his face, and it was to this glow that I came when my own spirits were low.

For six years he had lived on the same starvation diet, slept in the same airless and disease-ridden barracks as everyone else, but without the least physical or mental deterioration.[2]

"Wild Bill" told Ritchey the story of his life with his wife, two daughters and three young sons in the Jewish section of Warsaw, Poland:

When the Germans reached our street they lined everyone against a wall and opened up with machine guns. I begged to be allowed to die with my family, but because I spoke German they put me in a work group. I had to decide right then . . . whether to let myself hate the soldiers who had done this. It was an easy decision, really. I was a lawyer. In my practice I had seen, too often, what hate could do to people's minds and bodies. Hate had just killed the six people who mattered most to me in the world. I decided then that I would spend the rest of my life, whether it was a few days or many years, loving every person I came in contact with.[3]

Wild Bill suffered on the same starvation diet, surrounded by disease and despair. But he was totally different from the others—he experienced NO physical or mental deterioration! Why? What was the secret source of power that had kept this man emotionally well in the face of every torment? It was the power of unconditional love. He loved every person with whom he came into contact. He had learned the secret that negative thoughts lead to negative words, which lead to negative attitudes and emotions.

THE CHOICE OF MIRTH

DID YOU KNOW that the reason many grieving individuals over-come their loss and find happiness once more is simply because they choose to be happy? After bearing the heavy weight of grief for an extended period of time, most mourners decide they prefer joy and choose to move past their sorrow.

You may have suffered greatly in your life due to circumstances over which you have little control. But no matter what you have gone through and how much pain you have suffered—and are possibly still suffering—you always have the power of choice. Although it may be difficult, you can choose how you want to respond.

To illustrate, let me share the story of another Holocaust survivor. This man's name was Viktor Frankl, a Jewish psychiatrist who was imprisoned by the Nazis during World War II. His parents, his brother and his wife died in the camps or were sent to the ovens. He lived from day to day wondering if he would be next. Then one day, naked and alone in a small room, he began to become aware of what he later called "the last of the human freedom"—the one freedom his Nazi captors could not take away. Frankl realized that, no matter what the Nazis did to him, they could not rob him of his right to decide within himself how it would all affect him. He had the power to choose his response.[4]

Many individuals suffer unimaginable hardships. You may have experienced things that few others will ever understand. Nevertheless, no matter what has happened to you, your ability to choose your response remains your own. No one can take it from you.

Here is an even greater truth regarding this matter of choice: When you choose joy, God will help you to attain it! He will give you the power of spiritual joy for the asking.

The Bible says, "Give all your worries and cares to God, for he cares about what happens to you" (1 Pet. 5:7). Do you have deep hurts, wounds or grief you've never been able to overcome? Try this: Kneel down in prayer and, just as if you are lifting up an invisible present, physically hand your hurt or memory to God, asking Him to take it from you. Now thank Him for His great love and deliverance. You will begin to discover wonderful relief.

Now, make a fresh determination to choose joy. The Bible promises that God will give you joy and praise. When Jesus Christ entered the city of Jerusalem He proclaimed His mission by reciting Isaiah 61. Part of that passage deals with Christ's desire to give us spiritual joy.

> The Spirit of the Sovereign LORD is upon me, because the LORD has appointed me to bring good news to the poor.... To all who mourn in Israel, he will give beauty for ashes, joy instead of mourning, praise instead of despair.
>
> —ISAIAH 61:1, 3

A powerful saint named Corrie ten Boom used to say, "There is no pit so deep that God's love is not deeper still." The power of Jesus Christ is much greater than any bondage, sickness, sorrow or pain. Jesus said:

> Here on earth you will have many trials and sorrows. But take heart, because I have overcome the world.
>
> —JOHN 16:33

Here are some additional keys for developing a merry heart.

How to Develop a Merry Heart

How can you develop a heart that is filled with joy? What does it take to foster an internal environment that promotes good health and keeps away disease? Here are five important keys:

1. Practice forgiveness.

Who has wronged you or hurt you deeply? The first step in overcoming deadly emotions is forgiveness instead of anger, resentment and bitterness. Even if you don't feel it at all, forgive that person or persons as an act of choice. Unforgiveness rarely hurts anyone but the person who is holding it. So free your heart of that bondage and let a fresh stream of healing begin to flow inside of you.

> For if ye forgive men their trespasses, your heavenly Father will also forgive you: But if ye forgive not men their trespasses, neither will your Father forgive your trespasses.
> —Matthew 6:14–15, kjv

2. Take control of your tongue.

The words you utter have enormous consequences. The Bible declares, "Death and life are in the power of the tongue" (Prov. 18:21, kjv).

A transformed heart is the only guarantee that the words you speak will be uplifting. The Lord said, "For whatever is in your heart determines what you say" (Matt. 12:34).

Remember, what you speak sets in motion your future—and it affects your body. "Kind words are like honey—sweet to the soul and healthy for the body" (Prov. 16:24).

3. Surround yourself with positive friends.

Since words, thoughts and attitudes are contagious, choose your friends carefully. What can you expect if you surround yourself with people who spew negative stories, spread rumors or use language that is unbecoming? Scripture says, "Let your conversation be gracious and effective so that you will have the right answer for everyone" (Col. 4:6).

One of my cherished friends has had an incredible impact on young people—bringing thousands to Christ each year. I remember the day someone brought up an unfounded rumor about another ministry. Immediately my friend stopped the person and said, "I don't want to hear about it. I've made a decision to stop listening to gossip and rumor."

He is the kind of friend every person needs.

4. FEED YOUR MIND HEALTHY THOUGHTS.

It's important that we monitor what we listen to and watch. The Bible says, "Above all else, guard your heart, for it affects everything you do" (Prov. 4:23).

What enters our mind comes out in our actions—and affects our well-being.

Examine your television viewing, and make a commitment to turn off anything that harms your spirit. If that includes a favorite soap opera—so be it!

Stop listening to music that is depressing. Before you buy a CD, open the cover and read the lyrics. Is that what you want to pour into your heart, mind and soul?

I play praise and worship music at my office to promote healing in my patients. Anointed worship music can get into your spirit and fill your inner man with peace and joy. Why not try it? While you are driving or working, softly play anointed worship music. You will find that the peace of God will fill your heart.

What should occupy our thoughts? The apostle Paul offers this advice:

Fix your thoughts on what is true and honorable and right.
Think about things that are pure and lovely and admirable.
Think about things that are excellent and worthy of praise.
—Philippians 4:8

5. Meditate on God's Word.

When your heart is filled with Scripture, there's not much room for doubt or defeat.

You don't have to read five chapters a day to receive the benefit. Instead, start with just one verse, and meditate on it until the words flood your soul. Commit the words to memory so that you can call upon them at a point of need.

It's not the *quantity* of the Bible you read; it's the *quality*. Read a passage until you find a verse that speaks to your heart. Then read it again and again. Read it aloud. Form a prayer using that passage, thanking God for its truth in your life. In this way you can seek *revelation knowledge* from the Word. That's how God makes it come alive to you personally.

You will find that Scripture is an armor that will give protection from negative thoughts and emotions. It also creates faith within you.

A healthy mind that is full of love, joy, peace and forgiveness should lead to a healthy body. So *choose* to speak God-inspired words and think God-inspired thoughts.

Pay attention, my child, to what I say. Listen carefully. Don't lose sight of my words. Let them penetrate deep within your heart, for they bring life and radiant health to anyone who discovers their meaning. Above all else, guard your heart, for it affects everything you do.
—Proverbs 4:20–23

These spiritual keys can change your life—in fact, they can save your life! Scientists are just now beginning to document the power of our thoughts—both positive and negative. Karol Truman, a scientist and therapist who was studying the human brain and how thoughts affect it, believes that God can actually keep a record of our thoughts in heaven—just as the FBI can keep a record of our fingerprints in Washington. She recounts in her book, *Feelings Buried Alive Never Die,* the example of a lady with brain cancer who was close to death.

A group of scientists, including Karol Truman, arranged to monitor this woman to determine what would take place in the transition of her brain from life to death. They also placed a microphone in her room so that they could hear what she said at the time of death. The device they were using to monitor her brain had a needle pointing to zero in the center of a scale. Both the right and left sides were calibrated to 500 points, the left to negative and the right to positive.

Previously the device had been used to record the power used by a 50-kilowatt broadcasting station to send a message around the world. The needle had registered 9 points on the positive side.

As the very last moments of this woman's life arrived, she began to pray and praise the Lord. She prayed a beautiful prayer thanking God for His power and love and expressing her love for Him. The scientists became so engrossed in her prayer that tears began streaming down their faces as they listened.

Suddenly they heard a clicking sound on their forgotten device. The needle was registering a positive 500—and trying to rise higher as it bounced against the 500 positive post in its attempt. By actual instrumentation, the scientists had recorded that this woman's brain, alone and dying, yet in communication with God, had registered more than 55 times the power used by a 50-kilowatt broadcasting station sending a message around the world.

In another similar experiment, a man stricken with a deadly social disease was monitored by the same device. He verbally abused his attendant, cursing both her and God. The needle clicked back and forth against the 500 negative post. The scientists had established by instrumentation the positive power of God as seen in the woman and the negative power of the man's deadly emotions.[5]

If a person feeds on negative thoughts throughout the day, every task or every trial that comes his way will be approached from a defeated attitude before he even undertakes it. However, we have the ability, through the Word of God, to speak God's Word throughout the day and rewire our negative thoughts into positive thoughts, which will bring healing and health to the body and the mind.

It is my hope that as you follow these simple steps you will discover fresh joy, renewed zeal and the healing power of a merry heart. This sheds a whole new light on the scripture that says, "...bringing into captivity every thought to the obedience of Christ" (2 Cor. 10:5, KJV). For more information on this topic, please read my book *Deadly Emotions.*

DR. COLBERT'S CHECKLIST
FOR DEADLY EMOTIONS

⋏ Negative thoughts lead to negative words, which lead to negative attitudes and emotions.

⋏ Deadly emotions may prevent the body from releasing toxic material, especially from the liver and gallbladder.

⋏ Hatred and jealousy destroy the person first on the inside and then manifest in harmful actions and behaviors on the outside.

⋏ Many illnesses have been attributed to the deadly emotion of fear, including heart disease, depression, anxiety and mental illness.

⋏ The Word of God is an effective antidote in daily life for deadly emotions.

⋏ Godly thoughts will prevent the formation of deadly emotions.

⋏ Counteract nagging negative thoughts by speaking powerful, positive words and scriptures.

⋏ Choose to walk in love and forgiveness.

⋏ Choose to live in humility and gratitude.

⋏ Learn to laugh.

5

THE DEAD FOOD
DILEMMA

ONE OF MY patients, a home builder in his early sixties, came to my office for a physical exam. I discussed some danger signals I saw in his body and said, "If you don't make some changes, you're going to have problems down the road."

I compared his condition to a building and gave him this example: "Builders in a Third World country might be constructing a house out of concrete. Because there are no building codes, if they run out of concrete, they may try to finish the job with mud. Then, when a storm comes, the mud is washed away, and half the building caves in."

The same applies to our bodies. They must be built with strong materials.

What my friend didn't know about living foods was slowly killing him.

Since your body virtually is being remade every year, it needs to be reconstructed with vibrant powerful cells that can resist disease.

People come into my office every day sneezing and coughing—sometimes right in my face. Yet, because of what I put in my body, I have a high tolerance against disease.

You've probably heard it said many times, "You are what you eat!" Well, that's not quite true. The phrase should be, "You are what you digest and absorb."

That's why I tell people everywhere to eat *living* food—fresh fruit, fresh vegetables, nuts and seeds that still have their enzymes in them. At least half of your foods should be living, raw foods (or lightly steamed or stir-fried).

ENZYMES—YOUR SPARK PLUGS

YOU WERE CREATED with catalysts—called enzymes—that spark or speed up processes in our system by chemical reactions.

Your body is similar in some ways to the engine of a car. Every part must be in sync for it to operate properly. Let's say you have eight spark plugs, but only four of them are working. The car will still run, but roughly.

Enzymes are similar to the spark in the spark plug. When they are inhibited, your body is not going to function at peak capacity. I believe you can run on all eight cylinders instead of being exhausted.

There are three classes of enzymes:

1. Food enzymes
2. Digestive enzymes
3. Metabolic enzymes

Within those three categories are probably more than three thousand identified enzymes—and likely many more. They take proteins, fats and carbohydrates and structure them to form our body. Since we have *trillions* of cells, and approximately 97 percent are replaced every year, we must feed them properly. If we don't give them high-octane fuel, our cells may become weaker and weaker as they reproduce.

REPLACING YOUR CELLS

EVERY ONE HUNDRED twenty days our red blood cells are replaced. Every five to ten days the lining of our gastrointestinal tract is replaced with new cells. And every thirty days our skin is replaced as well with new cells. In some areas of our bodies the process is even faster. A corneal abrasion, for example, only takes two days to heal.

Are you beginning to understand why it's so important to feed your body living foods that contain the vitamins, minerals, nutrients, food and enzymes we need? As your cells die and are replaced, the new cells are totally dependent on the building materials available. If the materials are strong, you'll have a robust body, resisting disease.

Every tissue and organ—for example, the heart, lungs and kidneys—have their own unique enzyme system. That's why it's so imperative to eat a diet of living foods.

OVERCOOKED FOOD

OVERCOOKING YOUR FOOD can kill it. Dr. Edward Howell devoted nearly his entire life to researching enzymes. He found that when food is cooked at temperatures exceeding 118 degrees for thirty minutes, almost all the enzymes in the food are destroyed. These enzymes are the *living* part of the food.

When food is cooked until the enzymes have been lost, our bodies are forced to draw upon our metabolic enzymes—the raw materials and the spark that rebuild our bodies. In the process we start degenerating, which can lead to arthritis, heart disease, hypertension and immune problems that may even lead to cancer.

THE DEAD AMERICAN DIET

WHAT IS THE American diet? Processed, overcooked food. We eat hot dogs, French fries, hamburgers, baked bread—everything cooked, literally cooked to death. In other words, the life—the enzymes—have been cooked out of our food and destroyed.

Note carefully this important principle: *If we eat more raw, uncooked foods, our bodies will not need to expend their valuable metabolic enzymes to make digestive enzymes.* In other words, if you eat dead food, your body is still going to make the digestive enzymes it needs, but it's going to be expending vital metabolic enzymes needed for rebuilding our bodies; as a result, we won't have the strong, healthy immune systems that our bodies need to thrive.

Don't expend your enzymes. Eat more raw food. However, don't be tempted to rush to extremes. A balance of 50 percent raw and 50 percent cooked foods can be quite healthy.

Remember, your body is designed to use food enzymes to conserve your own enzymes. Raw foods contain enzymes to help us to break down our foods. Excessive cooked and processed foods will drain our metabolic enzyme potential and may leave excessive toxic waste in our colon, which could lead to a toxic colon, food allergies and degenerative diseases.

Think of it this way. We have an enzyme bank account. If you withdraw too much from the available balance, you're headed for trouble. I take a digestive enzyme with each meal to further supplement my enzyme bank account.

OVERDRAWING OUR ACCOUNT

YEARS AGO, I used to perform hair transplants. If a person came in who was nearly bald, I said, "You only have a few hairs I can transplant. You can only rob Peter to pay Paul so many times!"

It's the same with our metabolic enzymes. If we keep drawing on them to make our *digestive* enzymes (because we're eating only dead, cooked foods), then you know the result. Our bank account of metabolic enzymes will decrease, and our bodies will eventually become weaker and weaker.

Over the past century diets have changed tremendously, from eating mainly whole grains, fresh fruits and vegetables to eating excessive amounts of cooked meats, dairy, cheese, eggs, processed foods and sugar. As a result, disease has flourished.

Modern food processors have stripped our food of much of its remaining nutrients and destroyed the enzymes.

Dr. Weston Price, a dentist who studied native cultures in the early 1900s, was far ahead of his time. His research around the world showed that when refined, processed, cooked foods were introduced into various cultures, the people's health deteriorated rapidly—usually within only one generation. He noted that tooth decay and degenerative diseases such as heart disease, diabetes, arthritis and cancer increased at a level comparable to modern industrialized nations. However, when tribes and cultures remained on their native diet, they did not develop these diseases.[1]

The key to good health is to stay close to nature.

A CRAVING FOR SUGAR

THE AVERAGE CONSUMPTION of sugar in the United States jumped from 6 tablespoons a day in the mid-1980s to 16 tablespoons a day in the mid-1990s. That's an enormous increase in the consumption of sugar every day! The average American now consumes 150 pounds of sugar a year.

How is that possible? One Coke, Pepsi or soft drink contains about 10 teaspoons of sugar. Many kids drink three, four or five cans of soft drinks daily. These foods are dead and nutritionally depleted.

Many people resist the urge to add sugar to their foods. Yet they seem unaware of the amount of sugar they take in from hidden sources, including large amounts in cereals, ketchup and salad dressing. Canned fruit containing syrup is another source of sugar. You may think, *Well, it doesn't say sugar on the label.*

You're right. Looking at a nutritional label can be confusing. Instead of "sugar," manufacturers will use the terms "corn syrup," "dextrose" or "glucose." What you're consuming is sugar.

If you walk through any major grocery store, you will see aisle after aisle packed with beautifully packaged processed foods—chock-full of sugar.

Many people believe that a little sugar won't hurt them. Yet continuing to eat this "dead food" over and over can render serious results. Here are seven major problems associated with sugar.

1. DIABETES AND HYPOGLYCEMIA

Everyone knows that sugar is linked to diabetes.

It is also associated with hypoglycemia—low blood sugar. "How can I get low blood sugar by eating sugar?" When you consume sugar, the beta cells of the pancreas secrete the hormone insulin. Insulin lowers blood sugar levels and is necessary for your body to use glucose, which is used to produce energy. However, if excessive amounts of sugary foods are eaten (such as cookies, sodas or pies), excessive insulin may be secreted, which may drive the blood sugar too low. As a result, people may become shaky and light-headed due to low blood sugar.

2. OBESITY

Sugar is also a major cause of obesity.

A woman came to my office and said, "I've been on a low-fat diet and eat tiny meals, yet I'm gaining weight."

During our conversation I learned that throughout the day she was popping little sugar mints into her mouth to keep her breath fresh at the office. Without realizing it, she was consuming large quantities of sugar in the process. It was contributing to her weight gain.

I explained how the sugared mint was telling her pancreas to secrete insulin—a signal that says to the body, "Store fat! Store fat!" In other words, high insulin levels, which are caused from excessive sugar intake, will trigger the body to store fat. That's the reason most diabetics gain weight when they begin taking insulin—many times as much as twenty or thirty pounds. Insulin tells the body to store fat, and sugar triggers the pancreas to release more insulin. Many people are caught in this vicious cycle of eating sugar, which leads to elevated insulin levels, which then causes fat to be stored. Elevated insulin can also lead to low blood sugar and cravings for sugar. Thus the cycle starts over with the consumption of more sugar to prevent the symptoms of low blood sugar.

3. A DECREASED IMMUNE SYSTEM

Sugar also weakens our immune system by affecting the T cells, which protect us against viruses. It also temporarily impairs the B cells, which produce antibodies. It also impairs white blood cells called *phagocytes*, which protect us from bacteria. Eating 100 grams of simple carbohydrates (such as a few cookies, a large piece of cake or a few doughnuts) can reduce the ability of white blood cells to engulf and destroy microorganisms by 50 percent for a few hours. As a result, we are more prone to bacterial and viral infections.

4. BEHAVIORAL DISORDERS

Sugar is also associated with behavioral problems. There's a strong link between excessive sugar intake and attention-deficit hyperactivity disorder (ADHD). It is occurring with greater frequency because so many children have become "sugar-holics."

Some authorities have even linked sugar with criminal behavior. They believe that when individuals "come down" from a sugar "high," they become grumpy, irritable and sometimes violent. Grumpiness and meanness are commonly seen when the blood sugar is too low or when one is hypoglycemic.

5. OSTEOPOROSIS

Sugar can lead to vitamin and mineral deficiencies and osteoporosis, because it creates an acidic environment. The pH in our tissues decreases, and the body screams out, "Give me calcium!" If we do not have adequate calcium in our diets, our body may pull it from the bone to balance our pH, and we may develop osteoporosis.

6. YEAST PROBLEMS

We have already identified yeast as one of the dangers we face in our colon. Remember that yeast loves sugar. Everyone has some yeast in their intestines, but when we take in a great amount of sugar we may develop yeast overgrowth in the intestinal tract, and our abdomen may swell up like a yeast roll. When alcohol is added to the mix, we become like a brewery. A person with a "beer belly" is usually a product of sugar, yeast and alcohol.

Yeast infections, experienced by many women, are compounded by high intakes of sugar. For more information on this topic, refer to *The Bible Cure for Candida and Yeast Infections*.

7. SUGAR ADDICTION

The marketing of tobacco and alcohol has created millions of addicts. Now the same thing is happening with sugar. It is also highly addictive.

114

Many people start with eating a little cookie, and before long the entire box of cookies has been devoured. They can't control their craving.

The Bible places the drunkard and the glutton in the same category. "Do not carouse with drunkards and gluttons, for they are on their way to poverty" (Prov. 23:20–21).

The addiction becomes obvious when I put someone on a low-carbohydrate diet, treating them for yeast overgrowth. They often go through sugar withdrawals, becoming irritable and cranky. One husband phoned me, saying, "Dr. Colbert, you've got to do something. I've never seen my wife like this!"

Perhaps you recall the song, "Just a spoonful of sugar helps the medicine go down." Now we're coming to understand the hidden dangers in that sugar.

What's in the Bread?

Another dead food that deserves our attention is white flour.

Here is an experiment you need to try. Take a slice of white bread, place it in a small bowl and pour water on it. Almost instantly it becomes like paste. It's so much like paste you may be able to hang wallpaper with it!

Do you realize that piece of white bread may be doing the same thing in your colon? It's true. The paste you're eating may gum up your colon—causing constipation.

The manner in which processed white bread is made should give you food for thought. First, the outer shell is removed from the whole grain—with the healthy fiber and B vitamins.

Next, the germ is extracted. It contains the majority of the nutrients—vitamin E, the B vitamins and minerals. Both the shell (fiber) and the germ are marketed to health food stores, which speaks volumes.

What remains is the endosperm, or starch, which is ground into fine powder. But since it's not white, they add bleaching agents. The nutritional value is practically zero, so they add some inexpensive vitamins and minerals. If there's any life remaining, they cook it out, then market the remains as "enriched bread."

As a medical doctor, I am concerned that products advertised to build strong bodies can do just the opposite. When you are replacing your cells with white bread, you are constructing a fragile dwelling place. It's like adding a roof of straw rather than real shingles. What will happen when the storm winds blow?

We need to remember that breads, pasta and white rice are starches and are converted to sugars in our body. When you choose bread, be sure the words "whole grain" are on the label. It's the only way you'll receive the "goodness" that is processed out of most bread. Also look for brown rice and whole-grain pasta.

MALADIES FROM MEAT

THERE IS A reason Americans rank high in heart disease and cancer. We also score high in our consumption of meat. Those who live on hamburgers, steaks, pork chops and ham sandwiches are going to suffer the consequences.

I trained in a medical residency program operated by Seventh-Day Adventists. They are wonderful people who follow biblical health laws and live longer than most Americans. As a group they have some of the lowest incidences of heart disease and cancer. A great number are total vegetarians, eating no meat, fish, fowl, eggs or dairy products. Some are lacto-ovo vegetarians—meaning they sometimes eat eggs, drink milk and use other dairy products.

In my studies I became convinced that people with degenerative diseases such as diabetes, arthritis, cancer and heart disease should restrict their intake of meat and choose mainly chicken, turkey, fish and occasionally certified organic lean red meat. Eat meat only one time a day instead of the usual three times a day. Early research on the benefits of a vegetarian diet was conducted by Dr. Max Gerson, a doctor from Germany. Just after he finished medical school, he suffered from severe migraine headaches that would incapacitate him at least three days a week. The fellow physicians he consulted said, "When you reach forty-five or fifty-five years of age, the headaches will go away. There's nothing we can do."

Dr. Gerson turned to a study of nutrition to solve his problem. He began by saying, "If babies drink milk, perhaps I should go on a milk diet." He tried, but the headaches remained.

Next he looked at the diet of primates—monkeys in particular. They ate fruits, vegetables and nuts. He said, "Let me start with just eating apples."

Immediately, the headaches disappeared. So, in a controlled study, he began adding one food at a time to the apples to see what would trigger his headaches—different fruits, vegetables, dairy products and meats. If a headache appeared, he would eliminate that food from the list.

What resulted was the Gerson Plan, which not only cured most migraines, but also resulted in dramatic improvement of many patients with cardiovascular disease, arthritis, rheumatoid arthritis and lupus. Even some cancers went into remission. The diet is based on organic vegetables (primarily in juice form) and excludes all animal protein.

"No Way!"

REV. GEORGE MALKMUS, a Baptist minister from New York, developed colon cancer at the age of forty-two. It was a baseball-sized tumor. He had watched his own mother die a horrible death from colon cancer after surgery and chemotherapy. Doctors were ready to start him down the same path when he said, "No way!"

Instead, he consulted with a trusted friend who believed in a nutritional healing plan. Malkmus eliminated processed foods, sugar, meat and dairy products, and he lived on fruits and uncooked vegetables only. These are *living* foods. He began to drink one to two quarts of carrot juice every day. He also supplemented his diet with barley green, a food high in chlorophyll.

The results were amazing. His skin cleared up, his energy was renewed, and his cancer disappeared. Malkmus wrote an extremely helpful book based on his experiences, *Why Christians Get Sick.*[2]

PROTEIN OVERLOAD

CONSUMING EXCESS MEAT and protein (including milk products, cheeses and eggs) congests the organs and cells. It lowers the pH of the tissues, making the cells constipated from protein overload. When that happens, the cells become acidic and may not be able to adequately release their waste products, and the body may become overloaded with toxins. Since high-protein diets are so popular, I will discuss this in more detail in the chapter on dieting.

Earlier I told you of my bout with psoriasis. To this day, when I consume too much protein the condition breaks out. So I've learned to control my diet.

I am not on a crusade to have the world stop eating meat. However, people with heart disease, arthritis, cancer, psoriasis or some other degenerative disease need to know this information and should at least limit their meat intake.

When you choose to eat meat, always look for the leanest cuts—chicken breast, turkey breast or very lean cuts of filet mignon or tenderloin, which are preferably certified organic meats. Remember, the fatty portion of the meat is where most of the dangerous toxins are located. Many people order prime rib, not realizing that some cuts contain 50 percent fat or more.

You may wonder, *Where will I get my protein?*

A balanced diet that includes small amounts of lean meats and generous portions of legumes (beans) can give you the protein you need.

Many bodybuilders and dieters are ingesting large amounts of protein and harming their kidneys and other parts of their bodies. I was once guilty myself, and because my body could not process the excess protein, not only were my kidneys affected, but also my skin and joints. When I decreased the protein, the conditions cleared.

WHAT'S IN THE MEAT YOU EAT?

THE MEAT YOU'RE eating most likely contains chemicals—poisons that may be killing you. Few people think about the quantities of antibiotics in the meat they consume. Most chickens are given antibiotics, especially tetracycline, to counter salmonella and other bacteria.

In the past, it was common practice to give growth hormones and estrogens to animals in order to add muscle and bulk to increase their value. Fortunately, now these practices have changed. But pesticides are often present in the fatty tissues of the animal.

You may say, "Well, I eat fat-free meat." No, you don't. I guarantee that every piece of meat has some fat in it—including filet mignon, chicken breast and turkey breast. When you eat *any* kind of animal fat, the pesticides from the meat can go to *your* fatty tissue—and you reap the cumulative damage.

Always ask for certified organic meat. It's the safest you can eat.

THE TRUTH ABOUT MILK

"DON'T FORGET TO drink your milk!"

You probably heard that phrase a thousand times when you were young. Certainly milk is great for babies, or God would not have created women with the ability to breast-feed their children.

However, there is another side to the story. Most children I see with chronic ear infections, chronic sinus infections and many other conditions have dairy sensitivities. I take these youngsters off dairy products and substitute soy or rice milk; many times the problems clear up.

Do you realize that man is the only species in the animal kingdom to drink milk as an adult? When you consume cheese, butter and drink milk, you're often setting yourself up for problems, because many people have some degree of allergy or sensitivity to these foods.

Milk is pasteurized through heating, which changes the protein in such a way that our bodies may not be able to digest and assimilate it properly. As a result, we may develop allergies or sensitivities to it.

Many people believe they need milk to supply their calcium needs. When milk is pasteurized, the calcium becomes an inorganic form, which is less easily assimilated by the body. That's why many nutritionists recommend that you get your calcium from other sources. Soy, seeds or nuts are high in calcium.

Dairy sensitivities and allergies have been linked to skin rashes, eczema, ear infections, nasal allergies, chronic sinus infections, fatigue and spastic colon. If you (or especially children) have any of these, stop all dairy products—including skim milk, butter and even yogurt. Do it for one week or ten days, and watch the improvement. You then may decide to limit or avoid dairy products in order to relieve your medical condition.

SKIP THE SALT

SALT IS ANOTHER dead food you should avoid. Most Americans eat between 10 and 20 grams of salt a day. "But I don't use a salt shaker!" you insist. That doesn't matter—the salt is in your food.

Most of our food is processed, and it is loaded with salt. Why? Because salt is a preservative that prolongs the shelf life of the product in which it is used.

What does salt do inside our bodies? It may raise our blood pressure. Nearly one out of four Americans have high blood pressure—nearly sixty million people. I see patients with the problem every day.

What's the answer? I ask these people to stop eating processed foods (again, high in salt) and to drink eight glasses of filtered water daily. It usually has a positive effect on their blood pressure.

EGGS AND ALLERGIES

EGGS, LIKE DAIRY products, may cause allergies. They are a great source of protein, yet when they're cooked, the heating impacts the protein in such a way that you may not absorb or digest it well, and you may develop allergies or sensitivities to it.

An occasional egg is good for you, especially organic eggs or the new choice eggs, which contain omega-3 fats. Still many people can't handle eggs.

The "big three" food allergens are eggs, milk and wheat—usually in that order. Many people are allergic to the gluten in the wheat, which also is protein.

This is the destructive cycle that often happens. The duodenum, which is the first part of the small intestines, is many times irritated or inflamed from medications such as aspirin, antibiotics or anti-inflammatory drugs; excessive acid secretion;

etc. Thus, when a person consumes milk protein (casein), egg protein (albumin) or wheat protein (gluten), the intestinal barrier is compromised by being inflamed. Thus, whole food proteins such as casein, albumin and gluten may be absorbed directly into the bloodstream. The body may then produce antibodies to the proteins. As a result, we are wasting the body's immune system, which is fighting against something that's supposed to be helping us. It's like driving a car with a leak in the gas tank. The battlefield is the intestinal tract where the antigen (which is the food) meets the antibodies produced by the body. This antigen antibody reaction further damages the lining of our gastrointestinal tract, creating more food allergies and sensitivities. This becomes a vicious cycle.

I've seen people who are continually exhausted, with dark circles under their eyes, because they're allergic or sensitive to either milk, wheat, eggs or other food or inhalant allergens such as dust, mold, pollen or animal dander. When dairy, wheat and eggs are eliminated for seven to ten days, there is usually a marked improvement in their health. These foods may then need to be rotated in the diet every three to four days. For more information on this topic, refer to *The Bible Cure for Allergies*.

ALIVE, ALIVE

ARE YOU READY for your diet to be transformed into one that is vibrant and full of life? Here are four additional recommendations that will help the process:

1. CHECK YOUR OIL.

Every person should take in good fats every day. It's important for your heart, your skin, your hair and for every part of your body. Good oil is necessary because it nourishes and strengthens our cell membranes. I recommend 1 tablespoon of flaxseed oil once or twice a day, or you can take it in gelcap form. Keep the liquid form refrigerated; it is only good for one month after opening. Never cook with flaxseed oil. Evening primrose oil is also excellent and available at health food stores. Fish oil is another excellent oil. I take one capsule three times a day.

I also recommend extra-virgin olive oil, which is cold-pressed (not heated).

2. EAT NUTS AND SEEDS.

Nuts and seeds are other raw items we should eat. I regularly eat sunflower seeds, almonds and walnuts.

Some of the healthiest nuts are almonds, walnuts and hazelnuts. Almonds are excellent because they are high in monounsaturated fats and contain about 20 percent protein.

Initially, go easy with nuts and seeds, or you may have digestive problems. Start out light and gradually build up your system.

If you leave nuts unsealed for thirty days, they may become rancid, doing more harm than good. Package nuts in plastic containers or sealed bags and place in the refrigerator or freezer until you are ready to use them. Do your best to avoid salted and roasted nuts.

3. BUY A JUICER.

Personally, I drink one or two cups of fresh carrot juice practically every day. It's a great way to take in a tremendous amount of nutrition, plus I'm getting minerals in a usable state.

I encourage everyone to have a juicer. A drink of carrot and celery juice is great! It can also make a delicious soup. And remember this rule: *You should eat your fruits and juice your vegetables.* Juicing fruits can raise the blood sugar dramatically. If you have a Vitamix juicer, you can juice the whole fruit and vegetable. Thus you are also able to have the fiber, which prevents the blood sugar from rising dramatically.

Juicing allows the nutrients to be absorbed easily into your tissues. The benefits are delivered quickly to where the body needs them—much faster than taking a vitamin or mineral tablet.

Supplements are important to make sure our basic nutritional needs are being met, but you should make it a priority to eat adequate amounts of fruits and vegetables.

I counsel my patients, "Don't use the shotgun approach. Narrow and focus your supplements to exactly what your body needs—no more!"

4. TAKE A CHLOROPHYLL DRINK.

I recommend, and take, Green Superfood, which is a chlorophyll drink containing wheatgrass, barley grass, alfalfa, spirulina, chlorella and blue-green algae. It has plenty of chlorophyll, an important colon and blood cleanser. Most excellent chlorophyll drinks will have at least one of the four main chlorophyll-containing foods in them:

- Alfalfa—full of healthy minerals
- Barley grass—very high in chlorophyll
- Wheatgrass—contains *superoxide dismutase,* an important antioxidant enzyme
- Algae—filled with essential nutrients

Products with the commercial names of Green Superfood, Barleygreen, Progreens, Greens Plus, Blue-Green Algae, Chlorella or Spirulina are all excellent. They contain chlorophyll food with living enzymes. You can find these mixes at health food stores, through a nutritional doctor or by calling my office.

WATCH THE COMBINATIONS

BILLIONS OF DOLLARS are spent each year treating digestive problems. Often when there is a change toward a healthy diet, our systems are not prepared for the sudden switch, and there is gas, bloating and indigestion. That's why some people say, "I feel worse than before."

It's because our bodies are so toxic. Our system must become adjusted, and the best method is to learn the art of combining foods.

If you have a sensitive gastrointestinal tract, you may have candida overgrowth and should read *The Bible Cure for Candida and Yeast Infections*. Also, begin to practice food combining.

As far as food combining, it's best to eat fruits by themselves. When you eat fruits with proteins, starches and vegetables, they tend to ferment and cause problems. Remember, choose whole fruit over fruit juice since the juice tends to spike the blood sugar and can cause hypoglycemic problems. Also, eat the fruit between meals. If your children want a snack, give them a banana or an apple instead of sugar snacks.

Combine starches (potatoes, breads, pasta, corn, beans) and vegetables (salads, broccoli, cauliflower, green beans). They work great together. Again, this is for patients with a sensitive gastrointestinal tract.

Combining starch with protein, however, is one of the worst things you can do if you have a sensitive gastrointestinal tract. Why? The protein needs a highly acidic environment to digest it, whereas the starch needs an alkaline environment for digestion. For example, when you combine a baked potato with steak, or rice with pork chops, you're sending mixed signals to your digestive system. As a result, you may have fermentation and indigestion problems.

Remember, eat meats with vegetables, not with starches.

A DIET OF STRENGTH

SOMEONE RECENTLY REMARKED, "Dr. Colbert, can life really be sustained on fruits, vegetables and water?"

I remember visiting Busch Gardens in Tampa, Florida, and observing a giant gorilla. He was huge—with a massive chest and arms with bulging muscles.

What did the gorilla eat? No doughnuts, no candy, no cookies and no meat. This animal had a diet of bananas, fruits, vegetables and nuts, and he grew exceedingly strong.

WHAT THE BIBLE SAYS ABOUT LIVING FOODS

WHEN GOD CREATED Adam and Eve, they lived on fruit and vegetables—and during that time the life span was up to nine hundred years. Biblical scholars tell us that after the Flood, when people began eating more cooked foods and meat, their life expectancy decreased to about one hundred years.

Moses lived to be one hundred twenty years of age, and the Bible says that "his eyesight was clear, and he was as strong as ever" (Deut. 34:7). His vision was phenomenal. From the top of Mount Nebo, "the LORD showed him the whole land, from Gilead as far as Dan" (v. 1). That's a distance of more than one hundred miles.

The Old Testament also includes an amazing story regarding the benefits of healthy eating. The first chapter of Daniel records that the children of Israel had been taken captive by the Babylonians. The king instructed the master of the eunuchs to bring some of the children of Israel, some of the king's descendants and some of the nobles to be trained to serve in the king's palace. These were "strong, healthy and good looking young men...well versed in every branch of learning...gifted with knowledge and good sense, and have the poise needed to serve in the royal palace." They were taught "the language and literature of the Babylonians" (Dan. 1:4).

Among those chosen was Daniel, a brilliant young man from Israel's tribe of Judah. The king had prepared for them "a daily ration of the best food and wine from his own kitchens" (v. 5). These "delicacies," according to biblical scholars, were rich foods, including meats. The king believed this diet would cause these young men to become even wiser.

Daniel told the chief of the eunuchs he would refuse the king's food because he did not want to "defile himself" (v. 8). The chief, who was partial to Daniel, was worried and told him, "My lord the king has ordered that you eat this food and wine. . . . If you become pale and thin compared to the other youths your age, I am afraid the king will have me beheaded for neglecting my duties" (v. 10). His job was on the line, and he had to make sure these young men were healthy and mentally sharp.

Young Daniel made a proposal: "Test us for ten days on a diet of vegetables and water. . . . At the end of ten days, see how we look compared to the other young men who are eating the king's rich food. Then you can decide whether or not to let us continue eating our diet" (vv. 12–13).

At the end of ten days, those in Daniel's group "looked healthier and better nourished than the young men who had been eating the food assigned by the king" (v. 15). As a result, "the attendant fed them only vegetables instead of the rich foods and wines" (v. 16).

Who were the other three in Daniel's group? Shadrach, Meshach and Abednego (v. 7). Not only did they serve the king well, but "in all matters requiring wisdom and balanced judgment, the king found the advice of these young men to be ten times better than that of all the magicians and enchanters in his entire kingdom" (v. 20).

Never underestimate the power of a healthy living diet.

In the Bible, as in life, there are rules and principles we must obey. What is likely to happen to the person who defies the law of gravity by jumping off a building? If that person doesn't die, he or she will certainly experience pain and suffering. Disobeying the laws of nutrition (and the degenerative diseases that result) will surely have the same effect.

It is my hope that as you start eating more living foods, you will see the results in a healthier you.

DR. COLBERT'S CHECKLIST
FOR LIVING FOODS

⌁ Each year over 90 percent of your body is remade by the foods you eat.

⌁ Slow your eating process for proper digestion.

⌁ Don't consume cold drinks with food.

⌁ Eating too much protein taxes your system and creates an acidic environment.

⌁ Protect your enzymes by eating live foods.

⌁ Avoid overcooked and processed foods.

⌁ Increase your intake of raw fruits and vegetables.

⌁ Greatly reduce sugar consumption.

⌁ Eliminate white, processed bread from your diet.

⌁ Eat whole-grain breads.

⌁ Remember, eat your fruits and juice your vegetables.

⌁ Get protein from small amounts of meat and larger amounts of legumes.

⌁ You need oil every day. (Flaxseed, primrose, fish oil and extra-virgin olive oil are excellent.)

⌁ Have a chlorophyll drink daily.

⌁ For the sensitive GI tract, combine meats with vegetables, not with starches.

6

THE DIETING
DECEPTION

F OR YEARS YOU ate like a starving teenager, and now you're
paying the price. Your hips bulge, your thighs expand when you
sit, and you've developed "love" handles that aren't so lovely at all.

What is your solution? You fully expect to find your answer at
the grocery store. So you start by picking up "diet" cottage cheese
instead of the regular kind. You whisk your grocery cart to the
next aisle where you find diet yogurt. Of course, you musn't forget
the diet soda, which contains aspartame, and the diet ice cream,
which contains Olestra. Now for the low-fat popcorn, chips and
sugar-free candy bars. At the checkout counter you pick up a little
book that outlines the latest fad diet. There—you feel as if you're
well on your way to your former slender self.

But after several weeks of this diet you find you're feeling increasingly fatigued and grouchy, and you've actually gained weight. What happened? In this chapter, I'll explain how this weight gain may have happened. But in essence, you've been tricked by the dieting deception. And what you don't know may be killing you!

Even though most Americans have listened to the latest scientific research showing the perils of fats, sugars, high cholesterol, dangerous foods and a sedentary lifestyle, there is still a rise in obesity. According to the National Institute of Health, even though the dietary intake of fats and cholesterol is decreasing, the average weight of American young adults has increased by ten pounds. Before 1980 only one-fourth of the population was obese. Today, however, approximately one-third of the population is obese.

The reasoning behind many diet foods and fad diets is unwholesome, unnatural and can be quite dangerous. You see, the underlying philosophy involves never denying your taste buds, food urges or impulses, but rather deceiving your body into thinking it is getting all the sugar and fat it desires. But the deception doesn't work, so we get larger and consume more unhealthy products. Eventually, we sacrifice our good health on the altar of fad dieting.

There are hundreds of diet plans available in the marketplace. Most of us can use our common sense to avoid the obviously unhealthy plans—like eating only hot dogs or eating French fries on every even day and pork chops on every odd day. (Don't go looking for those two diets—I made them up!)

But what constitutes a good diet plan? In fact, is a diet even necessary? Should we be looking for a miracle short-term diet "cure" to take off—and keep off—the excess pounds we've accumulated over a lifetime?

There are some very good diet plans available today. Perhaps the diet plan that has received the greatest attention in recent years is the Atkins Diet, formulated by Robert C. Atkins, M.D., founder and medical director of The Atkins Center for Complementary Medicine. More than 20 million people worldwide people have used his book *Dr. Atkins' Diet Revolution,* published more than twenty years ago, to lose weight quickly and easily. The book remained on *The New York Times* bestseller list for over two years after it was first published. It is still one of only two diet books listed on the Top 50 best-selling books of all time.

Because this diet has been revolutionary in the field of nutrition and wellness, we are going to take a closer look at it in this chapter. There are many good points to the diet that I agree with. As a short-term diet plan to help an individual to lose a few unnecessary pounds quickly and easily, it is excellent. However, I believe that there are a few things about this diet plan—and any other diet plan—that must be thoroughly understood for it to be completely effective and safe over long-term usage.

By understanding and applying these additional nutritional guidelines, you will arrive at a plan for eating that is safe and effective over a lifetime of use. Let's begin to develop our understanding of these issues by taking a closer look at the basic Atkins Plan.

AN OVERVIEW OF THE ATKINS DIET

THE DR. ATKINS Web site gives this information on the diet plan:

> Atkins is an amazing diet where you will never go hungry again, yet still lose weight. This is not a gimmick; it has been around for decades now. Most people will lose ten to thirty pounds in the first month! How do they do it? Eat all the meat, cheese,

eggs, fats (like butter and oils) as you like. No calorie counting. The trick? Eliminate carbohydrates from your diet. The amazing thing is that you will feel better mentally and physically while doing this diet. You will find that your cravings for foods will go away, and comfort foods are no longer necessary. Another benefit that most people report is increased mental alertness, no more feeling sleepy after a meal!

The Atkins Diet is recommended by Dr. Atkins and his staff as a "lifetime nutritional philosophy, focusing on the consumption of nutrient-dense, unprocessed foods and vita-nutrient supplementation." The diet restricts processed/refined carbohydrates such as high-sugar foods, breads, pasta, cereal and starchy vegetables.

MAJOR BENEFITS OF THE DIET

The plan works on the principle that diets high in sugar and refined carbohydrates increase your body's production of insulin. When insulin is at high levels in the body, the food you eat can get readily converted into body fat.

Carbohydrates also leave you less satisfied than meals high in fats and proteins, causing you to eat more and get hungrier sooner.

Using this knowledge, the Atkins Plan recommends that its clients get off the insulin-generating roller coaster of the low-fat diet and start cutting down on carbohydrate consumption, especially of the worst offenders—sugar, white flour and other carbohydrate-based products.

The Plan promises that its clients will achieve "three wonderful results":

- You'll start to burn fat for energy.
- You won't feel hungry in between meals.
- Your overall health will improve, and you'll feel better.

There are many good points to this diet. Perhaps most importantly, it is a known fact that Americans are taking in way too much sugar. The average American consumes approximately 150 pounds of sugar a year.

Scientists are discovering more and more evidence about the harmful effects of too much sugar. One scientist reports:

> Sugar consumption is positively associated with cancer in humans and test animals. Tumors are known to be enormous sugar absorbers. . . . More plagues than heart disease can be laid at sugar's door. A survey of medical journals in the 1970s produced findings implicating sugar as a causative factor in kidney disease, liver disease, shortened life-span, increased desire for coffee and tobacco, as well as atherosclerosis and coronary heart disease.[1]

We are also eating way too many processed foods, especially white bread, pasta, potatoes, corn, white rice and cereals. The Atkins Plan recommends that no processed foods be eaten while on the plan.

IMPORTANT CONSIDERATIONS TO REDUCE LONG-TERM DANGERS OF ANY DIET PLAN

NO DIET PLAN—including the Atkins Diet—is, in my opinion, intended for the long term. There are risks associated with staying on a diet plan for an extended period of time. I think it is very important to understand the limitations of any diet plan and to make nutritional choices to balance any diet plan into a sound nutritional eating plan for life.

Using the Atkins Plan as a starting point, let's consider the nutritional choices that you should make to develop a healthy eating plan for life. For short-term weight loss, the Atkins Plan—

and others—can work and will give you the results you are looking for: weight loss, increased energy, muscle tone and a feeling of wellness. But for long-term healthy results, be sure to include these considerations in your eating plan.

MAKE GOOD CHOICES ABOUT YOUR MEAT INTAKE.

One of the problems I see with the Atkins Plan is that patients are eating way too many meats—especially fatty meats. Increased protein can make the body and tissues more acidic and can cause problems in eliminating toxins and detoxifying the body due to the high amount of protein. When the body is acidic, it doesn't release toxic materials from the cells as readily. Also, excessive protein intake may put a strain on the kidneys.

Fatty meats such as pork and fatty cuts of red meat may contain chemicals such as pesticides, antibiotics, hormones and other toxins that tend to store in the fatty tissues. As a person eats these fatty cuts of meat, the toxic materials may be stored in their bodies.

Most people on a diet plan that allows unlimited amounts of meat consume much more meat than is healthy. Men usually need only 4 ounces of meat or 20–30 grams of protein with each meal. Athletes will need more protein, based on their activity level. Women usually need only 2–3 ounces of protein per meal, or 14–21 grams of protein, based on their activity level and lean body mass.

Eliminate as much pork and red meat from your diet as you can. If you enjoy eating a small amount of red meat, choose free-range meat. Certified organic meats and most free-range meat come from organically grown cattle and chickens where pesticides are not sprayed on the fields that supply food to the animals.

In addition, always choose the leanest cuts of meat. The leanest cut of chicken or turkey is the breast. The leanest cut of beef is the tenderloin or the filet. Limit your intake of these meats to 4 ounces. Don't order a 24-ounce steak just because your diet plan allows you to eat all the meat you want.

DON'T EXCLUDE FRUIT IN YOUR EATING PLAN.

The Atkins Plan allows very little fruit. Most patients will avoid fruit while on the plan. This is because fruits contain a higher amount of sugar than vegetables. However, fruit is one of the best sources of important antioxidants, vitamins and minerals— especially of vitamin C.

There are three main types of simple sugars. These include:

- Glucose
- Galactose
- Fructose

Glucose is found in breads, cereals, starches, pasta and grains. Fructose is found in fruits, and galactose is found in dairy products. The liver rapidly absorbs these simple sugars. However, only glucose can be released directly back into the blood stream. Fructose and galactose must first be converted to glucose in the liver to gain entrance into the blood stream. Thus, they are released at a much slower rate.

The fructose that is found primarily in fruits has a lower glycemic index compared to glucose and galactose. With its slower absorption rate—and its high antioxidant, vitamin, fiber and mineral content—fruit is an important and healthy addition to your lifetime eating plan. If you limit your intake of fruit while you are trying to lose some weight quickly, be sure to add low-glycemic fruit back to your eating plan as soon as you reach your goal. However, avoid the higher glycemic fruits like dried fruits and bananas and avoid fruit juices. The lower glycemic fruits include berries (blueberries, blackberries, strawberries, raspberries), Granny Smith apples, kiwi, grapefruits, lemons and limes.

BE CAREFUL WHICH FATS YOU USE.

With the Atkins Plan you can actually overconsume protein foods, which usually contain a lot of fat. There are good fats and bad fats. Be sure that you are aware of which fats are bad for you, and decrease or eliminate them from both your short-term diet plan and your long-term healthy eating plan.

The bad fats are primarily saturated fats, trans fatty acids such as hydrogenated and partially hydrogenated fats and excessive amounts of polyunsaturated fats such as mayonnaise, salad dressings, heat-processed safflower oil, sunflower oil and corn oil. Bad fats also include other polyunsaturated vegetable oils, which are found in grocery stores.

Trans fats, or hydrogenated and partially hydrogenated fats, are prepared by taking polyunsaturated fat such as corn oil, heating it to a high temperature and using high pressure to force hydrogen through it until it is saturated. This process permanently alters the structure of the fat and forms an unnatural configuration called "trans-configuration." Trans fats have been found to be more harmful to your arteries than saturated fat, and they are implicated in heart disease and cancer. Many diet foods are "built" on trans fats, and so they really could be killing you.

Trans fatty acids are found in margarine, vegetable shortening and in most processed foods, including baked goods, pastries, cookies, cakes, pies, breads, processed peanut butter, many salad dressings, mayonnaise and many other foods. Read labels carefully, and avoid foods that contain hydrogenated or partially hydrogenated fats.

Choose foods that are rich in monounsaturated fats. These include the following:

- Extra-virgin olive oil
- Natural organic peanut butter
- Almonds
- Almond butter

- Avocado
- Olives
- Guacamole

- Organic peanuts
- Macadamia nuts

Other good fats include:

- Cold-pressed (not heat-processed) safflower, sunflower or sesame oils (found in most health food stores)
- Hazelnuts
- Organic butter in small amounts
- Fish oil
- Walnuts

- Brazil nuts
- Seeds and nuts
- Flaxseed oil

I do not recommend the use of canola oil as it contains trans fats. During the hydrogenation process of refining canola oil, trans fats, or trans fatty acids, are created. Trans fats, often referred to as the "deadliest fat in the American diet," have been linked to an increased risk of heart disease and cancer.[2] Researchers fear that the American people are putting their health at risk by consuming trans fats, as these fats raise the level of "bad" cholesterol while decreasing "good" cholesterol. Therefore, consumers are ingesting a substance that may be clogging their arteries and damaging their health.[3] Currently trans fats are not listed on product labels. However, hope is on the horizon as activists are working to implement laws that will require the labeling of trans fats, providing consumers with this important information.

BE SURE YOU ARE GETTING ENOUGH FIBER.

One of the main problems that I see with most diet plans—including the Atkins Diet—is that most individuals on the diet do not eat enough fiber. As a result, they become constipated. We need approximately 30–35 grams of fiber a day.

There are two types of fiber. Water-soluble fiber includes ground flaxseeds, oat bran, oats, carrots, beans, apple and citrus fruits. This type of fiber dissolves in water. There is also insoluble fiber, which does not dissolve in water. Insoluble fiber includes wheat bran and the skins of fruits and rooted vegetables.

Many fruits are a good source of soluble fiber, such as apples, pears and most citrus fruits. The fiber of citrus fruits found in the walls of the fruit is called pectin. When pectin is broken into smaller molecules, the body can absorb it better, and it has been proven to have capabilities to help prevent metastatic disease, which is the spread of cancer.

Carrots, beans, lentils, legumes and peas are good vegetable sources of soluble fiber.

Fiber intake is crucial. Fiber comes from many sources—vegetables, fruits, grains. Fiber and water are necessary to move waste through the colon smoothly and easily, thus reducing the risk of colorectal diseases like constipation, irritable bowel, diverticulosis, colon polyps, hemorrhoids and even colon cancer.

If you are having problems with constipation or desire to add more fiber to provide necessary colon-cleansing action, you may want to consider a fiber supplement. Some good sources of fiber that can be obtained through a fiber supplement include psyllium, ground flaxseeds, oat bran, wheat bran and modified citrus pectin. Look for these ingredients on the labels of food-derived fiber supplemental formulas that you can find at a health food store. It is helpful to take at least 1 teaspoon of fiber supplement thirty minutes before you eat with 8 to 16 ounces of water. This will help to cut your appetite and absorb fat. It may also prevent you from being hungry. Soluble fiber also helps to remove cholesterol from the colon by binding bile acids. It helps to control diabetes, too. It prevents colorectal diseases by speeding up the transit time in the colon, thus decreasing the time cancer-causing chemicals are in contact with the colon wall, probably decreasing the risk of cancer.

Remember that fiber is activated by water. Whenever you increase your fiber intake, the need for fluids increases. Anyone taking a fiber supplement should drink at least two quarts of water daily. Remember to drink your water thirty minutes before meals or two and one-half hours after meals. You may also drink small amounts of water with your meals—4 to 8 ounces.

EAT FOODS THAT ALKALINIZE YOUR BODY.

The combination of recommended foods on some diets—including the Atkins Diet—can cause your body to become too acidic. When the body is acidic, your body may try to buffer the acidity by pulling calcium out of the bones. In addition, your body will not release the toxins out of the cells easily, and they may become constipated with toxic waste. This will probably cause you to feel sluggish; you may be low on energy and may have a diminished mental capacity.

You will want to be sure your healthy eating plan includes foods and supplements that can alkalinize your body. The pH of your tissues is indicated by the pH of your urine, and it should be at 7. If it drops to 6, you are ten times more acidic than you should be. If it drops to 5, your tissues are one hundred times more acidic than they should be, and you may feel the symptoms described above. You can purchase urine pH strips at most drug stores.

Most vegetables and fruits are alkaline, so include many fresh vegetables and fruits in your diet. Add the low-glycemic fruits to your diet. I recommend that at least 50 percent of your diet consist of fruits and vegetables. Even though lemons, limes, oranges, berries and grapefruit are acidic outside the body, inside the body they are actually alkalinizing.

Drink lots of water, especially alkaline water, which alkalinizes the body and unconstipates the cells so that they will start releasing their toxins. You can add alkaline drops to the water or purchase an alkalizer water filter, which I highly recommend. (See Appendix.) Choose a lot of fruit and vegetables. Eat the fruit instead of drinking the juice, except for lemon or lime juice. I recommend 1 tablespoon of lemon juice in water three times a day to help to alkalinize your body. I also recommend fasting one time a week or at least one time a month.

Following is a chart of alkalinizing and acidic foods.

FRUIT

ACIDIC	ALKALINE	
Cranberries	Dates	Mangoes
Pomegranates	Grapes	Pineapples
Strawberries	Citrus fruits	Raspberries
	Apples	Blackberries
	Bananas	Apricots
	Cherries	Olives
	Peaches	Coconuts
	Pears	Figs
	Plums	Raisins
	Papaya	Melons

GRAINS

ACIDIC	ALKALINE
Brown rice	Millet
Barley	Buckwheat
Wheat	Corn
Oats	Sprouted grains
Rye	
Breads	

MEAT AND DAIRY PRODUCTS

ACIDIC	ALKALINE
All meats	Nonfat milk
Fish	
Fowl	
Eggs	
Cheese	
Milk	
Yogurt	
Butter	

NUTS

ACIDIC	ALKALINE
Cashews	Almonds
Walnuts	Brazil nuts
Filberts	
Peanuts	
Pecans	
Macadamia nuts	

SEEDS

ACIDIC	ALKALINE
Pumpkin	All sprouted seeds
Sesame	
Sunflower	
Chia	
Flax	

BEANS AND PEAS

ACIDIC	ALKALINE
Lentils	Soybeans
Navy	Limas
Aduki	Sprouted
Kidney beans	

Sugars

Acidic	Alkaline
Brown and white sugar	Honey
Milk sugar	
Cane sugar	
Cane syrup	
Malt syrup	
Maple syrup	
Molasses	

Oils

Acidic	Alkaline	
Nut oils	Olive oil	Corn
Butter	Soy	Safflower
Cream	Sesame	Cottonseed
	Sunflower	

Building a Healthy Lifetime Eating Plan

As I have previously mentioned, the majority of people in the United States eat too much fat, sugar and salt and not enough fiber in their diets. The keys to the ultimate healthy lifestyle are found in eating primarily fruits, vegetables, whole grains, nuts, seeds, beans, legumes and lean meats. Avoid refined sugar and flour; avoid bad fats, which include hydrogenated and partially hydrogenated fats, excessive amounts of saturated fats and heat-processed polyunsaturated fats and foods high in salt. Also limit your intake of red meat—choosing the leanest cuts possible.

There are five basic guidelines that I recommend for healthy eating. I want to give you those guidelines. Then I will briefly outline my recommended eating plan—the Carbohydrate-Protein-Fat Plan. Both these guidelines and the Carbohydrate-Protein-Fat Plan are expanded in my book *Walking in Divine Health*.

FIVE BASIC GUIDELINES

1. Reduce the intake of high-starch foods, including bread, processed cereals (this includes most cereals), crackers, bagels, pretzels, corn, popcorn, potatoes (including mashed, baked and fried), sweet potatoes, potato chips, corn chips, pasta, rice, rice cakes, Rice Krispies treats, beans and bananas by one-half to three-fourths.

2. Avoid all simple-sugar foods such as candies, cookies, cakes, pies and doughnuts. If you must have sugar, use Splenda or Stevia, a herbal sweetener that you can purchase at a health food store. Choose fruit instead of fruit juices.

3. Increase your intake of nonstarchy vegetables such as spinach, lettuce, cabbage, broccoli, asparagus, green beans and cauliflower. If you have reached your ideal body weight, you can eat beans, peas and lentils. If you have not reached your ideal body weight, eat starchy vegetables only in moderation.

4. Choose healthy meats such as turkey breast, chicken breast, fish and free-range beef. Select healthy fats such as nuts, seeds, flaxseed oil, extra-virgin olive oil or small amounts of organic butter. Use extra-virgin olive oil and vinegar as a salad dressing. Choose the healthy fats we have listed instead of hydrogenated fats, excessive amounts of saturated fats and heat-processed polyunsaturated fats. Remember never to cook or fry with polyunsaturated fats.

5. Eat three meals a day consisting of fruit, non-starchy vegetables, lean meat and good fat. You should also have a healthy midmorning, midafternoon and evening snack.

By following these guidelines I believe you will experience increased energy and improved health.

THE CARBOHYDRATE-PROTEIN-FAT PLAN

THE NUTRITIONAL PLAN I recommend to my patients is the Carbohydrate-Protein-Fat Plan. Here's how it works. Each time you eat, you should combine foods in a ratio of 40 percent carbohydrates, 30 percent proteins and 30 percent fats.

This program balances the correct ratio of carbohydrates, proteins and fats, and it controls insulin. Elevated insulin levels decrease physical performance and is one of the primary predictors used in evaluating a person's risk of developing heart disease. To simplify this program, in my book *Walking in Divine Health* I list the food categories and blocks, and then demonstrate how to use the blocks throughout the day.

For your planning here, let's look at some comparisons.

One block of protein is equal to 7 grams of protein, which is equivalent to approximately 1 ounce of meat such as beef, chicken breast or turkey breast.

One block of carbohydrates is equal to 9 grams of carbohydrates, which is equivalent to ½ slice of whole-grain bread, ¼ whole-grain bagel, ⅕ cup of whole-grain rice, ½ apple or ¼ cup of whole-grain pasta. Of course, choose most often the low carbohydrate choices such as fresh vegetables if you are trying to lose weight.

145

One block of fat is equal to 1.5 grams of fat, which is equivalent to ⅓ teaspoon of olive oil, 6 peanuts, 3 almonds or 1 tablespoon of avocado.

In this eating plan you will be getting much larger portion sizes than each individual food block. In fact, the average sedentary woman will get three food blocks at each meal, one food block midmorning, one food block midafternoon and one food block at bedtime. An active female who exercises three to four times a week for at least thirty minutes may have four food blocks with each meal and one food block between meals and at bedtime.

A sedentary male may have four food blocks at each meal and one food block between meals and at bedtime, whereas the active male who exercises three to four times a week may have five or six food blocks at each meal and one food block between meals and at bedtime.

Use this Carbohydrate-Protein-Fat Plan to establish your lifetime eating habits. You'll feel better, look better and live longer.

Use the following eating tips to make the plan a success.

EATING TIPS

1. Drink 8–16 ounces of filtered water thirty minutes before a meal, and take a fiber supplement that does not contain sugar.

2. Eat the protein portion of your meal first since this stimulates glucagon, which will depress insulin secretion and cause the release of carbohydrates that have been stored in the liver and muscles, which will help prevent low blood sugar.

3. Chew each bite at least twenty to thirty times, and eat slowly.

4. Never rush through a meal. Rushing will cause hydrochloric acid to be suppressed, making digestion difficult.

5. Never eat when you are upset, angry or bickering. Eating should be a time of relaxation.

6. Limit your starches to only one serving per meal. Never eat bread, pasta, potatoes, corn and different starches together at one meal. Choose low-glycemic carbohydrates such as vegetables. If you desire to lose weight, limit carbohydrates to one meal a day or avoid them completely. Never combine starches at a meal. This elevates insulin levels. If you do go back for seconds, choose fruits, vegetables and salads, but not starches.

7. Although it is best to avoid sweets, there will be special occasions such as birthdays, holidays and anniversaries when you will want to have a dessert. When you eat a sweet, simply eliminate the starch or the bread, pasta, potatoes and corn. Have only a small dessert. However, be sure to have your protein and fat to balance out the sugar in the dessert. Don't eat desserts regularly.

8. Avoid alcoholic beverages, not only because alcohol is toxic to our bodies, but also because it triggers a tremendous insulin release and promotes storage of fat.

The Keys to Digestion

THE MANNER IN which we break down food is essential to proper digestion. The best method is to chew our food thoroughly. Yet in this high-speed society, we grab a snack on the run and gulp it down with an oversugared drink.

Slow down!

In reality, digestion begins with *thinking* about food and with feeling hungry. Those thoughts and emotions start the digestive juices flowing. It's called the *cephalic* phase of digestion.

It is extremely important to approach a meal in a state of calmness, peacefulness and thankfulness. A person who is experiencing anger, hostility, strife or fear will likely experience bouts of indigestion usually due to undersecretion of digestive juices. The Bible tells us, "A dry crust eaten in peace is better than a great feast with strife" (Prov. 17:1).

Not only is there a spiritual benefit to saying grace before a meal, but also there is a physical benefit. Always take a moment before eating to take a deep breath, release all your tension and give thanks. Now you're in the *mood* for good digestion. Through hormones and enzymes, your body directs the signals to the digestive system and says, "It's time! Be prepared!"

CHEW, AND CHEW AGAIN

Properly chewing your food is not just good manners; it is vital to your health.

First, learn to take small bites and eat slowly. Some nutritionists recommend chewing everything at least twenty to thirty times. To me, the numbers are not as important as making sure you chew until the food is thoroughly mixed with saliva.

Your saliva contains a special enzyme called *ptyalin*. Plus, it has an ingredient named *amylase,* which digests carbohydrates.

If you fail to chew your food well, and it is not properly broken down into small pieces, the outside portion of the food is digested but the inside portion is not.

What happens to the "unchewed" portion? It goes down the gastrointestinal tract and may begin to ferment into a toxic material. You don't want to think about the next step. Overgrowth of bacteria can develop, rotting and fermenting the food, resulting in bloating and gas. Your body must deal with these large chunks of food it has not adequately digested. This can lead to food sensitivities or allergies, intestinal toxicity, overgrowth of unfavorable bacteria, yeast overgrowth and impaired intestinal permeability.

DRINK WITH MEALS?

Our culture has taught us to drink liquids when we eat. You'd be better served, however, to change that practice.

Research has shown that the best time to drink is thirty minutes before you eat and two hours after you eat. Why? There are three reasons:

1. Drinking fluids with your meal dilutes and flushes out the enzymes.
2. It may put a strain on your digestive tract.
3. Drinking cold liquids slows down digestion.

Your body actually "heats up" to help digest food. A glass of a cold beverage is dousing the heat and slowing down digestion. Your stomach has to heat back up to 98.6 degrees or higher to properly digest your food. If you need fluids with your meal, drink only small amounts, and choose something at room temperature.

DIGESTING THOSE PROTEINS

Protein digestion occurs mainly in the stomach by the enzyme *pepsin*. Before it can be activated, however, you need hydrochloric acid, which works on the enzyme pepsinogen, converting it to pepsin.

The main thing to remember is that you need acid in your stomach to activate the pepsin that digests the protein. Millions of people take antacids or other medicines such as Tagamet, Zantac, Pepcid, Axid, Prilosec and Nexium. Each of these acid-inhibiting drugs alters digestion. As a result, many people's digestive systems are not properly digesting proteins or absorbing needed nutrition. We need protein to have a strong immune system and to rebuild our muscles and physical structure. What is the consequence of inadequate digestion? Weak, unhealthy cells.

It is true that many people over the age of fifty are lacking hydrochloric acid—the "gasoline" of digestion. Patients over fifty should address the problem by taking supplements of hydrochloric acid if they have no active gastritis, ulcer or reflux disease. This should be under the direction of a nutritional doctor. You can start with 150 milligrams of Betaine HCL with each meal and gradually increase it. It is important that you be under the direction of a nutritional doctor, because if burning occurs in the upper abdomen, that is a sign that you are taking too high a dosage of hydrochloric acid. But don't forget the benefits of eating slowly, chewing slowly and drinking before and after your meal—and only a small amount of beverage (4 to 8 ounces) with a meal. Preferably the beverage should be water.

By following the important considerations and guidelines in this chapter, you can establish healthy eating habits that will increase the success rate of any short-term diet plan you may choose to follow to lose weight. And your long-range nutritional plan will be everything that you need it to be to ensure your excellent health for many years to come. Eat for health and life!

DR. COLBERT'S CHECKLIST
FOR DIETING

⋏ No diet plan was intended to be the only way a person should eat for the rest of his or her life.

⋏ Increased protein can make the body and tissues more acidic and can cause problems in detoxifying the body.

⋏ Fruit is one of the best sources of important antioxidants, vitamins and minerals.

⋏ When you are trying to lose some weight, avoid the higher glycemic fruits (i.e., dried fruits and bananas) and avoid fruit juices.

⋏ Fiber—crucial in our bodies—comes from many sources such as fruits, vegetables and grains. We need 30–35 grams of fiber a day.

⋏ Pectin, the fiber found in the wall of citrus fruits, is broken into smaller molecules that the body absorbs; it has proven capabilities to help prevent metastic disease.

⋏ Choose foods that are rich in monounsaturated fats like extra-virgin olive oil, natural organic peanut butter, almond butter and avocado.

⋏ Be sure your healthy eating plan includes foods and supplements that can alkalinize your body.

⋏ Use the Carbohydrate-Protein-Fat Plan to establish your lifetime eating habits.

⋏ Chew your foods until they are thoroughly mixed with saliva.

7

THE DEPLETED
SOIL DISASTER

~ハ~ハ~ハ~ハ~ハ~ハ~ハ~ハ~ハ~ハ~ハ~ハ~

D ON'T FORGET TO eat some dirt!" I recently told the participants at a health seminar. I was only *half*-kidding.

You and I are made of flesh, blood and bone, yet in reality we
are products of the earth. "And the LORD God formed a man's
body from the dust of the ground and breathed into it the breath
of life. And the man became a living person" (Gen. 2:7).

What happens to our body when our life on earth is complete?
It is finally reduced to a few pounds of mineral dust. Back to
where it began!

Minerals are vital to our survival and are the building blocks of
life. Without them our immune system begins to fail, and we may
develop disease as we slowly begin to degenerate.

EARTH'S ESSENTIALS

DO YOU REMEMBER the large chart on the wall of your chemistry class? It's called the "periodic table," and it lists the 103 minerals found in our earth's crust.

Of this list, twenty of the minerals have long been established as absolutely essential for life—and needed on a daily basis. Eight are "macro minerals," meaning we need plenty of them—over 100 milligrams a day. These eight are calcium, magnesium, phosphorous, sodium, potassium, chloride, sulfur and silicon.

The remaining twelve are *trace* minerals, of which we need only small amounts daily—less than 100 milligrams. They include zinc, copper, cobalt, iodine, manganese, chromium, vanadium, selenium, molybdenum, boron, tin and iron.

Due to the findings of current nutritional research, they may eventually be expanding the list of essential minerals. Many experts add lithium, rubidium, nickel, bromine, barium, fluoride, strontium and even arsenic. You may wonder, *How could arsenic be essential?*

It may be essential, but only in tiny, trace amounts—and again, this isn't proven.

There are also toxic minerals—the ones with which you have to be extremely careful, since excessive amounts can be deadly. These include mercury, lead, cadmium, aluminum and increased levels of arsenic.

Our bodies are unique. They have the ability to produce many of the needed vitamins, but try as we might, we are unable to create minerals. We have to depend on the soil.

Minerals come from the earth, are absorbed into plants and become part of our food. It's also a fact that if we sow in mineral-depleted soil, the needed nutrients won't be present, and we will not have strong bodies.

Because of soil erosion, the discontinuation of crop rotation, manuring, mulching and other factors, much of our land has been depleted of minerals and left with three basic minerals: nitrogen, phosphorous and potassium. Other minerals may be present in small amounts, but the fertilizers we are using are causing our soil to be reconstituted and filled mainly with these three.

Again, when we eat foods grown on depleted soils, we are not getting the needed minerals.

Many Americans, from cradle to grave, have a serious mineral shortage. We like to believe that our toddlers are getting all the calcium they need from milk, yet many are commonly deficient in calcium and zinc. Many teenagers are consuming inadequate amounts of calcium, magnesium, iron and manganese. And many adults (especially women) don't get enough iron, calcium, magnesium and zinc.

Without question, I believe that mineral deficiency is a major factor in the increased levels of disease in the United States.

LOST THROUGH PROCESSING

EARLIER WE DISCUSSED the problems of processed foods, and the danger grows even larger when we examine the vital minerals we are losing.

Most food is processed so it won't spoil quickly. In the processing of our food, many of the nutrients are cooked out. Our food is then placed in a can or package to be frozen. Then large portions of salt or sugar are usually added to make sure the shelf life is extended for as long as possible.

Bread that is milled falls into the same category. In the process of milling bread, over 75 percent of the chromium, manganese, magnesium, potassium, iron, zinc and phosphorous is lost. And over half of the copper, calcium and molybdenum is stripped away. Think of it! In the milling and processing of bread we lose a great percentage of essential minerals. Add that loss to our depleted soils, and you begin to understand why we are being physically weakened.

THE PICA FACTOR

I BELIEVE THIS depletion of minerals will often lead to a condition called *pica*—defined as an abnormal craving to eat substances not fit for food, such as clay, chalk, paint chips or even ice, which can damage your teeth by chewing it. Research is being conducted on this phenomenon.

Many are convinced that since many Americans do not get the minerals they need, they are turning to sugar and salt to satisfy their cravings. As a result we have an epidemic of high blood pressure, heart disease and diabetes, and we have become an obese society.

Certainly other issues are involved, but the pica factor must be addressed.

ARE YOU GETTING YOUR "MACROS"?

OF THE EIGHT "macro minerals" essential in our bodies, two are required (and usually present) in relatively large amounts: calcium and magnesium.

Approximately 99 percent of our calcium resides in our bones and teeth. The remaining 1 percent is circulated in our blood. The importance of calcium in our bones and teeth is for structural purposes, but its presence in our blood supply is to regulate muscle contraction, heart contraction and nerve function.

What happens when we don't supply calcium to our bodies on a daily basis? That 1 percent in our blood doesn't sound like much, but if it is not present, a tragic series of events is triggered. We start "cannibalizing" our bones, actually *sacrificing* our bones to put calcium into our bloodstream. Why? Because the heart demands to beat—even at a major cost to our body. Our system will always choose the performance of muscle and heart contraction and nerve function over bones.

This robbing of our bones leads to osteoporosis, which literally means "porous bones"—or bones lacking in minerals and mass. Approximately one out of four postmenopausal women develop osteoporosis, and the number is increasing. So that we do not develop this condition, calcium and phosphorus must be present in amounts that balance each other.

THE PHOSPHORUS-CALCIUM BALANCE

THE AMERICAN DIET is high in phosphorus—a macro mineral quite similar to calcium. It's important that phosphorus be balanced with calcium. For every 1 milligram of calcium, we should have only 1 milligram of phosphorus.

The average person eats far too much meat, which contains ten to twenty times more phosphorus than calcium. For instance, 3½ ounces of meat have about 200 milligrams of phosphorus, but only about 10 milligrams of calcium.

Soft drinks are also a problem. The average soda contains about 50 milligrams of phosphorous, yet it contains virtually no calcium. Most people are taking in huge quantities of phosphorus and only small amounts of calcium. This imbalance causes more calcium to be lost in our urine, leading to the formation of kidney stones and contributing to our epidemic of osteoporosis.

There's another danger. The phosphorus can push the calcium out into the soft tissues, forming *soft tissue calcification*. It may eventually cause plaque and calcium to build up in the arteries, leading to coronary artery disease and vascular problems.

This is one of the reasons a diet high in meat and low in calcium

156

is extremely dangerous in the long term. Again, I'm not asking you to become a vegetarian; just make a determined effort to cut back on your meat intake.

Unfortunately, many low-carbohydrate diets such as the Atkins Diet recommend eating significant amounts of meat, which will raise the phosphorus level and lead to increased calcium excretion. This in turn can contribute to the epidemic of osteoporosis.

The Role of Magnesium

ANOTHER NUTRIENT THAT needs to be balanced with calcium is magnesium. For every 2 milligrams of calcium, we need at least 1 milligram of magnesium—an essential nutrient that is deficient in a great number of people.

Magnesium helps to pull the calcium out of the soft tissue, making it more soluble. This assists in preventing kidney stones and hinders calcification in the arteries and in the soft tissues. It is also a cofactor for over three hundred different enzyme reactions in the body. It helps prevent muscle spasm, heart attacks and heart disease, aids in lowering blood pressure and eases asthma. It also helps prevent osteoporosis.

Foods rich in magnesium include nuts, seeds, dark green leafy vegetables, grains and legumes. It's easy to see why our teenagers are deficient in this mineral, because they rarely eat these foods. A quality multimineral supplement will supply us with our daily requirement.

Calcium-Robbing Foods

FOODS HIGH IN oxalates, such as spinach and chocolate, bind calcium in the intestines. Sure, spinach is good for you, but too much of anything can be harmful.

Oxalates can actually prevent us from absorbing calcium. That's why chocolate milk is not a good choice if you need calcium, since it can prevent calcium from being absorbed and can also cause kidney stones.

Here's something else I strongly recommend. Do not take fiber with your calcium. Phytic acid, found in whole grains and fiber, can bind the calcium and prevent it from being absorbed.

CALCIUM-RICH FOODS

THE RECOMMENDED DIETARY allowance (RDA) for calcium is about 1,000 milligrams for the average person and 1,200 milligrams for menopausal and postmenopausal women. Foods highest in calcium are milk products, yet there is a concern over the fat content and also because many people have allergies and sensitivities to milk products. Thus, milk may be doing more harm than good. Try choosing low-fat, sugar-free, plain yogurt, and add your own fruit to it. Or drink skim milk—you'll get about 300 milligrams of calcium per 8 ounces. Other foods high in calcium are almonds, broccoli and soy beans.

Most of us, because we take in so much phosphorus, need a calcium supplement. The best calcium supplements available are *chelated* calcium supplements. Chelated minerals are minerals such as calcium that are bound to an amino acid or other substance, which improves their absorption. Chelated calcium supplements include calcium aspartate, calcium malate and calcium citrate.[1]

Many calcium supplements such as Tums (calcium carbonate) depend on stomach acid for absorption. Unfortunately, many men and women over fifty don't produce enough acid, so they may be wasting their money. Therefore, much of the calcium in Tums may not be absorbed.

To help prevent osteoporosis:

- Take a chelated calcium supplement or a chelated calcium and magnesium supplement.

- Make sure your daily multivitamin contains vitamin D (400 units a day), boron (2 milligrams a day) and magnesium (400 milligrams per day).

- Eliminate sugar and caffeine since they increase calcium loss.

- Decrease your protein intake so you don't have high phosphorus levels. Limit meat to 6 ounces a day. Even better, eat meat only one time a day.

- Exercise regularly.

- Avoid alcohol and cigarettes.

- Eat foods high in calcium, such as broccoli, almonds, soybeans and skim milk products, provided you are not allergic or sensitive to them.

Note: Menopausal woman should be on a natural progesterone supplement. The word *natural* is extremely important. I recommend Natural Change Cream by Nutri-West. You can order it by calling (800) 451-5620.

More Macros

IN ADDITION TO calcium, magnesium and phosphorus, the eight macro minerals include the following:

- *Potassium* plays an important role in the transmission of electrical impulses in our body. We take in plenty when we eat fruits—especially bananas.

- *Sodium* should be decreased since there is far too much salt added to most processed foods.

- *Chloride* is present in our cells and helps with our cognitive functions and nervous system. Foods high in chloride include egg yolks, milk, legumes and whole-grain cereals. Americans rarely are deficient in chloride due to their high intake of salt, which is sodium chloride.

- *Sulfur* is a vital mineral that helps form our tissues and activates enzymes. Good sources are meats, dairy products, beans and peas.

- *Silicon* is essential for skeletal growth and development. You can find significant amounts in whole-grain breads, cereals, beets and bell peppers.

BIG BENEFITS FROM TINY MINERALS

WHAT WE CALL "trace minerals" may only be needed in small amounts, yet they are vital to many chemical processes in the body. Here are the twelve we need on a daily basis:

1. IRON

Women need about 18 milligrams of iron per day—and are commonly deficient.

Iron is in the central core of the hemoglobin, which is the oxygen-carrying portion of the red blood cell. It's essential. If iron is not present, you may become anemic, which may lead to tiredness, sickness and fatigue—with greatly reduced energy levels.

I advise any woman who is exhausted and pale to see a physician. Have the doctor check your complete blood count (CBC), iron and ferritin level. Ferritin levels are reflective of the body's iron stores. If your iron or ferritin level is low, and if you are anemic, then you definitely need an iron supplement. Supplements are strongly recommended for teens and most menstruating women. During one menstrual period a woman may lose about 30 to 40 milligrams of iron, which needs to be replaced.

Foods high in iron include kelp, brewer's yeast, molasses, wheat bran, sesame seeds and wheat germ.

Remember, the same things that bind calcium also bind iron— and they include phytic acid, which is present in many fiber supplements.

We have been led to believe that liver is high in iron, yet all of the foods just mentioned have a higher concentration of iron. I sternly warn people not to eat liver. It's an organ meat, which means it filters out the toxins in an animal. If you want to eat a concentration of toxic residue, order liver the next time you go to a restaurant.

Chelated irons such as iron aspartate are easy to absorb. Also, ferrous fumarate and glycinate are easy on the gastrointestinal tract but are best absorbed on an empty stomach.

Vitamin C enhances the absorption of iron in a dose of 500 milligrams with each meal. The RDA of iron is 18 milligrams a day. However, if a woman is iron deficient, I will place her on 100–150 milligrams of ferrous fumarate with 500 milligrams of vitamin C two times a day for about a month. I will then recheck her complete blood count, iron and ferritin levels after being on this regimen for one month. The most commonly prescribed form of iron is ferrous sulfate, which commonly causes constipation and other side effects. Choose one of the chelated forms of iron listed above.

Men, except those with anemia, don't need extra iron. Anemia in a man usually indicates a problem of the gastrointestinal tract. A man with anemia should seek immediate medical attention since it usually means bleeding in the gastrointestinal tract— stomach, esophagus, intestine, colon, rectum or anus.

Iron can be a two-edged sword, because excessive amounts can cause oxidative damage to cells and organs. That's why men, as well as postmenopausal women, should not take an iron supplement unless they are anemic.

2. ZINC

Zinc is important to the formation of many enzymes in the body. It is also critical for supporting the immune system, fostering the insulin function and for the male sex organ.

We need 30 milligrams of zinc a day, yet the average person consumes only 10 milligrams.

Zinc should be balanced with copper—fifteen parts zinc to every one part copper. We also need to know that zinc and copper *antagonize* each other. If we take a lot of zinc, we will reduce the copper in our body, which can be harmful.

Zinc, copper and manganese are part of one of the most potent antioxidant enzymes in our body called *superoxide dismutase* (*SOD*). It is important to have adequate zinc, manganese and copper on a daily basis to assure adequate amounts of SOD. SOD then helps prevent damage to our cell membranes and our mitochondria membranes.

3. COPPER

A deficiency in copper is related to a decrease in energy production, decline in immune function and lower concentration.

Like iron, copper needs to be carefully controlled. Too much copper can cause oxidative damage to your tissues. Look for it on the label of your multivitamin/multimineral supplement. You can also get it from whole-grain bread, cereals, nuts, beans, peas and dark green leafy vegetables. A good comprehensive multivitamin should have about 2 milligrams of copper, and it should be properly balanced with 30 milligrams of zinc.

4. MANGANESE

Don't confuse manganese with magnesium. They are different. Deficiencies of manganese are associated with weakness, growth retardation and bone malformations. You can find this trace mineral in spinach, beans, peas, nuts, whole-grain bread and cereals. The RDA is 2 milligrams a day, but I recommend at least 5–7 milligrams of chelated manganese a day. This should also be found in a comprehensive multivitamin and mineral supplement.

5. IODINE

This mineral is needed to make thyroid hormones—vital for the growth and development of virtually every part of your body. Excellent sources of iodine include saltwater fish, kelp, onions and milk products. You need at least 150 micrograms a day.

6. CHROMIUM

Here's a mineral that helps maintain normal blood sugar levels, regulates insulin and may help control blood sugar in diabetics and patients with hypoglycemia. Chromium deficiency is very common, and the average American diet has inadequate amounts of chromium. Could this be one of the reasons why the incidence of diabetes is increasing? I believe so.

We need about 200 micrograms of chromium a day. Sources include whole grains, whole-grain bread and cereal. Chromium is commonly deficient in our diets because of the depletion of this mineral in our soil. GTF chromium, known as glucose-tolerance-factor chromium, is a good choice of chromium.

7. VANADIUM

Both chromium and vanadium are important in glucose and insulin metabolism. They have a positive effect on normalizing blood sugar for both hypoglycemia and diabetes. The recommended

daily amounts for vanadium have not been established. The esti-
mated requirement is around 10 micrograms a day.

Food sources of vanadium include black pepper, celery seed,
fenugreek seed, seafood, kelp, grains, meats and dairy products. I
recommend that you take a multivitamin that contains at least
100–200 micrograms of chelated vanadium due to the over-
consumption of sugar and processed foods and the rising
incidence of diabetes.

8. SELENIUM

To help protect cell membranes from free-radical damage and
to enhance your immune system, take selenium. It also aids in preventing *cardiomyopathy*—a disease of the heart muscle that
causes weakness of the heart. We find selenium in whole wheat,
brown rice and oatmeal—but only if they are from plants grown
in soils that contain adequate amounts of selenium. We need
about 100 to 200 micrograms of chelated selenium a day.

9. MOLYBDENUM

Our body requires between 50 and 150 micrograms of this mineral daily—more than most multimineral formulas contain.
Molybdenum is found in whole grains such as wheat, barley, rye
and millet, leafy vegetables such as spinach, lettuce, turnips and
mustard greens, legumes (beans and lentils) and milk. You can take
up to 500 micrograms of chelated molybdenum a day. This can be
found in a comprehensive multivitamin and mineral formula.

10. BORON

This mineral is essential for normal calcium and bone metabolism. You can find boron in fresh fruits, vegetables and nuts. We
need about 3 milligrams a day. Boron-containing foods include avocado, hazelnuts, pistachios, soy meal, apples, apricots, bananas,

pears, plums, broccoli and carrots. I recommend a comprehensive multivitamin and mineral containing 3 milligrams of boron.

11. TIN

This may sound strange, but we get enough tin from the residue that reaches us from tin cans. No additional supplement is necessary.

12. COBALT

You will have plenty of cobalt in your system as long as you take a multivitamin with B_{12}, which is cobalamin.

THE KEY TO TAKING AND REPLACING MINERALS

I AM CONSTANTLY asked, "Dr. Colbert, what is the best way to get the minerals I need? Is the answer in eating the right food? Or do I need a mineral supplement?"

I wish I could tell you that certain foods contain everything necessary for your daily intake of macro and trace minerals. They don't—and you know the reason why: depleted soil and mineral-deprived processed foods.

The best way to take and replace minerals is by taking a comprehensive multivitamin with a *chelated* mineral supplement.

A chelated mineral is simply a mineral that is bound to an amino acid. Some examples include products with malate, aspartate, ascorbate, citrate, fumarate, succinate, glycinate, lysinate and acetate (which are all amino acids). Don't worry about those technical terms. Just remember *chelated*.

Choose a supplement that is easily absorbed: soft gels, liquids, powders or quick-dissolving tablets. Some tablets contain high amounts of magnesium stearate, and often people have difficulty breaking them down—and they are sometimes not as well absorbed from the gastrointestinal tract.

Take your vitamin and mineral supplements with a meal—and look for one that you can take two to three times a day. The ingredients are needed throughout the day—not just at one time.

I am frequently asked, "Won't any popular multivitamin or multimineral do the trick? Isn't one as good as another?"

Recently, I examined the label of one of the most popular multivitamins sold in America, and here's a sample of what I found:

- *Calcium.* We need around 1,000 milligrams a day. It had 162 milligrams—in the form of calcium phosphate. Remember, we don't want a lot of phosphate, and calcium phosphate is poorly absorbed.

- *Magnesium.* We require up to 400 milligrams a day. It had 100 milligrams—in the form of magnesium oxide. Remember, oxide is poorly absorbed.

- *Copper.* We need up to 2 milligrams a day. Yes, it contained 2 milligrams, but in a poorly utilized form, cupric oxide. Again, oxide is poorly absorbed. Cupric oxide is a salt and is not nearly as well absorbed as chelated copper.

- *Manganese.* The RDA is 2 milligrams a day. It contained 3.5 milligrams in the form of manganese sulfate, which is poorly absorbed.

- *Zinc.* We need up to 30 milligrams. It contained 15 milligrams—in the form of poorly absorbed zinc oxide.

- *Chromium.* We should have about 200 micrograms a day. It contained only 65 micrograms. Plus, it was in the form of chromium chloride, again poorly absorbed.

- *Selenium.* We need up to 200 micrograms a day. It had only 20 micrograms—in the form of poorly absorbed sodium selenate.

- *Boron.* We should have about 3,000 micrograms per day. It contained only 150 micrograms.

- Two minerals in adequate amounts were iodine and molybdenum.

Now we can add popular multivitamins and multiminerals to our list of deficiencies. Not only are they lacking in nutrients, but they are delivered in forms that are often poorly absorbed.

What's the answer to finding the best supplement? Start by making a list of the amounts of each mineral you need, and read the labels or product literature until you are satisfied. I developed my own product line, Divine Health Nutritional Products, so that these requirements would be met.

WHAT ABOUT COLLOIDAL MINERALS?

A WOMAN CAME to my office and, with great excitement, said, "I don't need to take any vitamins or minerals. I'm on colloidal minerals!" She pulled a bottle from her purse and said, "Look, I get ninety different minerals in this bottle."

Colloidal minerals are simply a mixture of clay and water. To date there is no documented proof to the claims of colloidal minerals, and I have some reservations concerning their use. Some colloidal mineral products do not actually contain all the minerals listed on the labels. Also, many contain excessive amounts of toxic minerals—including mercury, lead, cadmium, aluminum and arsenic.

One of the greatest dangers of taking colloidal minerals is the large amount of aluminum we receive at the same time—and the levels are rarely listed.

Remember, toxic minerals will block out *essential* minerals. That is why it is vital for you to take a quality, chelated, balanced multvitamin, multimineral formula containing the twenty essential minerals every day.

Don't worry about eating a little dirt—just be certain it's the right kind.

DR. COLBERT'S CHECKLIST
FOR MINERALS

⋏ Because of soil depletion, we rarely receive all the minerals we need from foods.

⋏ Avoid toxic minerals, including mercury, lead, cadmium and aluminum.

⋏ Vital minerals are usually lost through food processing.

⋏ Our bodies require calcium (1,000 grams a day) and magnesium (400 milligrams a day). Lack of calcium leads to osteoporosis.

⋏ Magnesium assists in preventing kidney stones, osteoporosis and other maladies.

⋏ Women need more iron than men.

⋏ We need 30 to 50 milligrams of zinc each day.

⋏ Take 200 micrograms of chromium each day.

⋏ We need 100 to 200 micrograms of selenium a day.

⋏ We need 50 to 150 micrograms of molybdenum a day.

⋏ Supplement with 3 milligrams of boron daily.

⋏ Take 2 milligrams of copper daily.

⋏ Take at least 2 milligrams of manganese a day.

⋏ Colloidal minerals have not been proven effective.

⋏ Take a balanced multivitamin and chelated multimineral containing essential minerals every day.

8

THE RISK OF
FREE RADICALS

I AM DEEPLY SADDENED by cancer—especially when I talk with
people in their thirties and forties who are riddled with cancer.
Why should this be happening when we are promised "three score
and ten years," or seventy years of life? (See Psalm 90:10.) One out
of two people in the United States will at some time develop cardiovascular disease. One out of three people will develop cancer.
What we don't know about free radicals is killing us.

If we don't take preventive measures on this contaminated globe,
we may succumb to the same diseases that are afflicting millions.

Oh, how I wish I could tell you there is a pill available that will
prevent these dreaded diseases, but there's no such medicine. The
good news is that there are steps we can take to ensure that our
chances of developing heart disease and cancer are minuscule.
And in the process, we may even slow down the aging process and
prevent wrinkles.

Good Guys vs. Bad Guys

To win a major war you must first identify and locate the enemy. The number one adversary we face is *free radicals*. We have already mentioned them briefly, but they deserve closer scrutiny.

Free radicals are the *bad guys,* and antioxidants are the *good guys.* Unfortunately, we have left the gates open to the enemy soldiers and have not employed the forces to defeat them.

Virtually all of our organs and tissues are under constant attack by free radicals that are like biological terrorists ripping through our bodies. What are they? They are highly reactive molecules, produced in the body either by normal metabolic functions such as breathing, by taking medications or from toxins.

The dangerous free-radical-producing toxins include cigarette smoke, air and water pollution, stress and certain harmful foods—especially fats. Since we are all exposed to pollution in some form, there's not a person on earth who is immune from the threat.

Each free radical has an unpaired electron in its outer field that, if not "paired," can rip through the tissues. Think what would happen if a large crane were driven through the streets of Manhattan with an uncontrolled wrecking ball swinging from side to side. The skyscrapers may not fall, but they would be severely damaged. That's similar to what a free radical can do to your cells.

Since our bodies contain about sixty to one hundred trillion cells, you may wonder, "How can free radicals do serious damage?"

Each of those cells has a lipid "fatty" membrane around it—intended to form a shield to prevent it from harm. The free radicals, like that wrecking ball, can start ricocheting off the cell membranes—causing damage the body must somehow rush to repair.

When your body is inundated with free radicals without an armor of antioxidants to absorb them, your cell membranes are being damaged and may be destroyed. The free radicals begin to ravage the proteins, enzymes and then the genetic material—the nucleus where our DNA is formed. The mutations caused in the nucleus can result in cancer.

When free radicals begin their movement, they can initiate a perilous chain reaction—boom, boom, boom—and enormous damage is done. That's why they must be stopped quickly.

Here are two ways free radicals enter our body.

1. OXYGEN

One of the major "introducers" of free radicals is oxygen.

Oxygen is healthy and necessary. We can live perhaps five weeks without food, five days without water, but only about five minutes without oxygen.

Oxygen is vital, yet it has a dark side. Oxygen free radicals occur just by breathing; however, excessive amounts of these free radicals occur when we are exposed to air pollution, cigarette smoke, etc. The four main types of oxygen free radicals that are produced in our bodies include singlet oxygen radicals, lipid peroxide radicals, hydroxyl radicals and superoxide radicals. Each of these damages and may destroy tissues. Almost immediately, the biological structures start becoming rancid—similar to leaving butter out in the air. The deterioration begins.

2. FATS

Certain types of fats cause excessive free radical formation:

- *Polyunsaturated fats*—These fats are found in mayonnaise, salad dressings and in many types of oils, including sunflower, safflower and corn oils. Unfortunately, these fats we thought were so good for us are easily turned into rancid fats when they are combined with oxygen. Polyunsaturated fats have two or more double bonds between carbons, whereas monounsaturated fats have one double bond. Saturated fats have no double bonds between carbons. Since polyunsaturated fats have increased numbers of double bonds, they are more susceptible to lipid peroxidation, which forms significant numbers of free radicals in the form of lipid peroxide radicals. Therefore, it is easy to see that if you eat a lot of salad dressing or mayonnaise or use a lot of corn, sunflower oil, safflower oil or other polyunsatured fats, you can form tremendous amounts of free radicals. Thus the free radical damage continues.

· *Hydrogenated fats*—These fats include margarine, most commercial peanut butter, vegetable shortenings and shortening oils. For years we were taught to use margarine because it's vegetable oil, and most everyone believes that vegetable oil is healthier than butter or other forms of saturated fat. Hydrogenated fats and saturated fats both make platelets more sticky, increasing the risk of a clot, which could lead to a heart attack or stroke. However, the hydrogenated fat is much more dangerous since it interferes with essential fatty acid functions; saturated fats do not. Hydrogenated fats also change the permeability of cell membranes, which impairs the cell membranes' protective function.

These two forms of fat are in far more products than you see on the shelves of your grocery store. You'll find them in processed food, pastries, baked goods and at Taco Bell, Burger King and McDonalds.

Don't despair because you might have to give up some of your favorite foods. Later we will talk about some great alternatives that act to eradicate free radicals.

EFFECTS ON AGING

I'VE SEEN PATIENTS in their twenties whose skin is sagging. You can see it in their faces and arms.

"What did you have for breakfast?" I ask.

"Oh, I had a toaster pastry," one young woman replied.

"And what about lunch?"

"I ate at Pizza Hut," she replied. The previous night she had eaten a microwave dinner.

When I asked about eating fruits and vegetables, drinking plenty of water and taking vitamins and minerals, she said, "I'm still young! I don't worry about all that healthy stuff."

Yet on her face I could see the damage that had already begun.

Some of the most tragic cases of nutritional abuse I have seen are bodybuilders. In their quest to become strong, they are making unhealthy choices, and it shows. Many are taking steroids and growth-enhancing drugs—causing free-radical harm to their bodies.

Alcohol is also a major contributor to cell corruption. That's why heavy drinkers age much faster.

Far too many young people, when they reach drinking age—and before—begin smoking and abusing drugs and alcohol. These factors, along with sleep deprivation from staying out late, increase the free-radical function in their body. They start

174

damaging cell membranes, which results in early aging and degenerative diseases.

Later, perhaps at age thirty, they look at themselves and say, "I'd better change my diet and start exercising." Yet significant damage has already occurred. However, with proper nutrition, rest and avoiding toxins such as cigarettes, drugs and alcohol, some of the damage can be reversed. But without proper knowledge, a person may continue to produce excessive amounts of free radicals by choosing the wrong foods and lifestyle, resulting in accelerated aging.

THE PROBLEM OF STRESS

Dr. Robert Eliot, an outstanding cardiologist and author of the book *Is It Worth Dying For?*, coined the term *hot reactor*.

The hot reactor is someone who reacts with a dramatic increase in blood pressure and pulse over the most insignificant stressor. An example is a situation where one driver cuts off another in traffic. Suddenly, the second person has "road rage"—stomping on the accelerator and shouting obscenities. The blood pressure of the hot reactor shoots sky high.

In a research project at the University of Central Florida while I was in residency at Florida Hospital, we had university students in their late teens and early twenties play video games while we monitored their blood pressure. After a stressful game, we asked them to do "serial sevens"—starting at one hundred and counting backward by seven until they got to zero—while being monitored. The hot reactors would show a marked increase in heart rate and blood pressure. These are people who spend a dollar's worth of energy for a two-cent problem.

These same hot reactors are also forming excessive free radicals, which predisposes them to cardiovascular disease.

TOO MUCH EXERCISE

DR. KENNETH COOPER, the father of aerobic exercise who founded the world-famous Cooper Clinic in Dallas, discovered that some marathon runners were developing brain cancer. The finding presented a dilemma. Long-distance runners were considered to be extremely healthy, with practically no body fat. How could it be that these athletes could develop brain cancer?

Here's what was found. Exercise releases free radicals. The harder you exercise, the more you release large amounts of free radicals. If they are not quenched with antioxidants, they may cause destruction of cells, tissues, nuclear material and DNA—and they may form cancer. Recent research has linked free-radical activity to cardiovascular disease, many forms of cancers and cataracts.

I remember when my father was having cloudy vision. He visited an ophthalmologist who found he was developing cataracts. Dad phoned me, asking, "What should I do?"

"Are you taking the antioxidants I sent to you?" I wanted to know.

"No, I really haven't," he confessed.

I said, "Well, start taking them just as I told you: two tablets of antioxidants and three tablets of vitamin C twice a day—every day."

Less than three months later he returned to the eye doctor, and the cataract problem was totally gone. Unfortunately, these results do not always occur, but if you have cataracts that have just started to form, as my father did, then high doses of certain antioxidants may be extremely effective.

ACCELERATED AGING

OTHER CONDITIONS THAT are associated with free radicals include chronic fatigue, strokes, heart failure, ulcer disease, rheumatoid arthritis, asthma and Parkinson's disease.

Perhaps you have read about *progeria*, a rare disease that causes accelerated aging in children. A boy of ten or twelve can appear to be an elderly man—with balding gray hair, sagging, wrinkly skin, a frame bent over with arthritis and heart disease that goes with aging.

For years this disease has puzzled medical science. Now we know that progeria is caused by an inherent absence of internally produced antioxidant enzymes. In some cases, supplements of antioxidants have stopped the progression of the disease in certain forms.

FINDING THE ANSWER

HOW CAN YOU counter the effects of free radicals in your body? You can do so through antioxidants. Antioxidants are compounds that help protect against free-radical damage. They are able to disarm free radicals and break the vicious cycle. Oxidation is the process that leads to free radical formation. So by using an antioxidant, we are stopping the enemy in his tracks, blocking his steps.

There are two main types of antioxidants: those made by the body and those taken in by the foods and vitamins that we eat. Yes, our bodies actually make antioxidants. That's why children with progeria develop that rare disease—their bodies aren't manufacturing the antioxidants.

HOW YOUR BODY HELPS

THE ANTIOXIDANTS THAT our bodies produce include superoxide dismutase (SOD), glutathione and catalase. As long as you are living a healthy lifestyle, these antioxidants will keep most of the free radicals in check—up to a certain point.

How do we get the raw materials necessary for these antioxidants to function properly in our body? Let's look at each of them.

1. SUPEROXIDE DISMUTASE (SOD)

SOD is made from three basic minerals: copper, zinc and manganese. We need to take in these minerals every day to maintain a proper SOD level.

- Copper and manganese come from whole grains and nuts.
- Zinc comes from meat, egg yolks, milk, oatmeal, nuts and legumes.

Both children and adults are often deprived of these minerals (sometimes by choice) and need a multivitamin and mineral supplement. It is preferable to use a comprehensive multivitamin with chelated minerals.

2. GLUTATHIONE

This bodily manufactured antioxidant is extremely important and essential for life because it helps to protect the cell membranes. Yet it is vital that we give the body the necessary materials to make glutathione. Glutathione-rich foods include cabbage, broccoli, brussels sprouts, asparagus, avocados and walnuts. To ensure that we get adequate amounts, we need to take a sulfur-containing amino acid such as L-cysteine or N-acetyl cysteine, known as NAC. Reduced L-glutathione may also be taken in a dose of 250 to 500 milligrams, two to three times a day. This, however, is much more expensive than NAC and may not be absorbed as well.

NAC is much better absorbed than L-cysteine. L-cysteine is found in egg yolk, garlic, broccoli, oats, onions, wheat germ and yogurt. A supplement containing 500 milligrams of NAC daily is generally sufficient. NAC is needed to make glutathione, which is a main antioxidant in the tissues throughout the body.

Glutathione can neutralize free radicals many times before it (the glutathione) is oxidized; it also restores vitamin C and vitamin E to their reduced form so that they can continue scavenging free radicals. Glutathione also helps repair DNA and prevents free-radical damage to the DNA. Selenium acts as a cofactor with glutathione. Selenium is necessary for the production of enzymes needed to make glutathione.

NAC deactivates acetaldehyde, a chemical formed in people who drink alcohol and present in women who have recurrent yeast infections and candida of the intestines.

3. CATALASE

This enzyme in skin converts various peroxides and free radicals into oxygen and water. It also converts hydrogen peroxide to water. Catalase oxygenates the epidermis, resulting in smoother, younger skin.

ANTIOXIDANTS FROM FOODS AND VITAMINS

WHAT'S THE BEST strategy to attack the forces that invade your body? There is not one plan, but many. Let's begin with vitamins.

VITAMIN C

Dr. Linus Pauling, who won two Nobel prizes and died at the age of ninety-three, is best remembered for his research into vitamin C. After writing *Vitamin C and the Common Cold*, he was practically ostracized by the scientific and medical community. They could not believe that megadoses of this vitamin was a remedy for both colds and cancer.

Years later, vitamin C has proven to be a vital antioxidant. I recommend it to all my patients because it is one of the body's major antioxidant protectors, and it helps to restore vitamin E to its full potency so that it can continue to quench free radicals.

This vitamin should be taken with your meals—approximately 250–500 milligrams three times a day. And for those who are ill or have a degenerative disease such as osteoarthritis, I recommend doses of 1,000 milligrams three times a day. Of course, always consult with your physician. The RDA for vitamin C is only 60 milligrams—but I do not believe you will receive adequate antioxidant protection from such a small dose.

A cup of orange or grapefruit juice contains about 100 milligrams of vitamin C. One papaya has about 188 milligrams of vitamin C. One 8-ounce glass of acerola juice from India contains 3,800 milligrams, but acerola juice is hard to find and rather expensive. The best alternative is to take supplements.

Here's an interesting fact. About one million people die each year in the United States from cardiovascular disease—and about twelve million worldwide. Yet animals rarely die of heart disease. Why? Because nearly all animals have the ability to manufacture vitamin C in their bodies. Man doesn't. As a result, I believe this is one of the reasons why we have an epidemic of cardiovascular problems.

Most people believe that by taking one small tablet of vitamin C we receive all we need. Not true. We need it in sufficient amounts throughout the day.

I believe that the best type of vitamin C to take is buffered vitamin C, or mineral ascorbates. This vitamin is better absorbed in capsule or powdered form.

Some people, however, use tablets that are so hard you can't even break them with your fingers. They contain magnesium sterate, making them extremely hard and difficult to digest.

If you take a chewable vitamin C (recommended for children), be sure it doesn't contain sugar or NutraSweet.

Some tablets contain *sorbitol*, which is not a problem in small doses. However, if you begin taking 3,000 milligrams of vitamin

C with sorbitol, you are likely to have cramping, abdominal pain and gas. You may think you have the symptoms of a virus. That's why you should start out slowly. Your children will be protected with chewable vitamin C containing sorbitol in a low dose—100–250 milligrams.

Always rinse your mouth after taking vitamin C, since the acids can eat the enamel off your teeth. Better yet, brush your teeth after taking this vitamin.

As I stated before, a recent study of vitamin C has shown a high link between high doses of vitamin C pills and hardening of the arteries. I believe this is due to elevated iron or ferritin levels in these individuals. Vitamin C increases absorption of iron, and elevated iron causes more oxidation and free-radical damage to the lining of blood vessels, leading to plaque formation. If your iron or ferritin level is elevated, do not take high doses of vitamin C. Reduce your intake of iron-containing foods such as red meat, beef liver, fortified breakfast cereals, pumpkinseeds, blackstrap molasses, soybean nuts and spinach. Follow up with your doctor, and regularly donate blood until your iron and ferritin levels are normal.

Here is a list of selected iron-rich foods with their approximate iron content in milligrams:

- **Animal foods (meats)**
  Lean meats (3½ oz.): 3.0 mg.
  Chicken (3½ oz.): 1.1 mg.
  Cod fish (3½ oz.): 1.1 mg.
  Chicken liver (3½ oz.): 8.4 mg.

- **Egg yolks** (1 medium): 1.0 mg.

- **Dried beans or peas**
  Kidney beans (3½ oz. cooked): 2.4 mg.

Peas (3½ oz. cooked): 1.8 mg.
Lentils (3½ oz. cooked): 2.1 mg.
Garbanzo beans (3½ oz. cooked): 3.0 mg.

· **Vegetables**
Mustard greens (½ cup cooked): 1.8 mg.
Green beans (½ cup cooked): 0.4 mg.
Broccoli (½ cup cooked): 0.6 mg.

· **Fruits**
Raisins (½ cup): 1.8 mg.
Prune juice (1 cup): 3.0 mg.

· **Grains**
Iron-fortified cereals (read labels) (1 cup): 18.0 mg.
Oatmeal, instant (6 oz.): 6.3 mg.
Whole-wheat bread (1 slice): 0.8 mg.

· **Miscellaneous**
Blackstrap molasses

NOTE: Your body absorbs iron from animal foods more easily than from other foods.

VITAMIN E

Vitamin E, found mainly in seeds, nuts and vegetable oils, is also an important antioxidant. Sadly, in the processing of vegetable oils, most of the nutrients are lost, so always take extra vitamin E.

This vitamin decreases oxidation of lipid membranes, guards the heart and the blood vessels against oxidation by free radicals and protects the tissues of the breast, liver, eyes, skin and testes from oxidation.

Vitamin E is also a fat-soluble vitamin—working in the fatty compartments of the body, especially the cell membrane.

Vitamin C, on the other hand, is a water-soluble vitamin.

Vitamin E decreases blood clotting, which further reduces the risk of heart disease. Cardiologists are now recommending what we've known for years: "Take vitamin E."

The RDA for vitamin E is only 30 international units a day. However, I believe we need at least 400 to 600 international units—and possibly even more for diseased states. Some physicians recommend 1,600 units a day.

Start with 400 units, and increase the amount only after consultation with a competent nutritional doctor.

Before you purchase a vitamin product, be sure to buy a natural vitamin E that is made from plants rather than from petroleum products. Avoid the synthetic form of vitamin E, which comes from petroleum. It is recognized on the label as the "dl" form. It is called "dl-alpha tocopherol" or "dl-alpha tocopheryl." Natural vitamin E is called "d-alpha tocopherol" or "d-alpha tocopheryl."

Mixed tocopherols not only contain the d-alpha tocopherol but also contain d-beta, d-gamma and d-delta tocopherols for even greater antioxidant protection. Unique E is a product that contains the mixed tocopherols.

Wheat-germ oil contains vitamin E, yet only has about 20 units per tablespoon. One ounce of sunflower seeds contains only 14 units, and 1 ounce of almonds has only 10 units. It's impractical to take in 400 units a day from these sources. That's why I recommend a supplement.

VITAMIN A

Much has been written about the supplement beta carotene, which is converted in the body to vitamin A.

As you may know, carotenoids are responsible for the red, yellow and orange pigment in fruits and vegetables. Foods high in this nutrient include sweet potatoes, carrots and tomatoes.

In Finland, research was conducted in the 1980s on twenty-nine thousand men who were smokers. In the double-blind study, some of the participants were given beta carotene and others given a placebo (or a sugar pill).

The results were surprising. Those on beta carotene were doing *worse* than the patients on the placebo. So the National Cancer Institute repeated the study in the United States. The results were essentially the same. Those on beta carotene supplements had more lung cancer and a higher death rate than those on the placebo.

As a result, some doctors were saying, "Antioxidants don't work. Forget about them!"

Here was the problem. The tests were using a *synthetic* beta carotene capsule—and the participants were smokers. Remember, smoking is probably the worst free-radical-producing activity there is.

The best form of carotenoids (like beta carotene) is from fresh fruits and vegetables, such as carrot juice, which also contains beneficial alpha carotene. Studies have shown that alpha carotene is a much more potent antioxidant than beta carotene.

Also lycopene—found in tomatoes—is more active than beta carotene.

We can't just take an antioxidant pill and get the protective effect. We need to see the entire picture. Certainly beta carotene is a fairly good antioxidant. However, if you are a smoker, and you think antioxidants can prevent you from developing heart disease, cancer or early death, you're wrong.

Vitamin A helps night vision and promotes healthy skin. The acne medicines Retin A and Accutane are derivatives of vitamin A.

Be careful of the dosage. Too much vitamin A can cause

headaches, swelling of the brain, nausea, vomiting, dry skin, hair loss and liver damage.

I've had people come to my office who were losing their hair—only to learn that they were taking excessive amounts of vitamin A. If you take over 25,000 units (not beta carotene, but vitamin A), and develop any of the symptoms above, then that is too much for you. A pregnant woman taking that much runs the risk of having a baby with birth defects.

I recommend only 5,000 units of vitamin A per day. However, you won't have a toxic buildup if you are juicing carrots, which contain carotenoids. The trouble often comes from too much cod liver oil (containing concentrated vitamin A) or from vitamin A supplements.

SELENIUM

The nutrient selenium is more than a mineral. It's a component of glutathione, a very important antioxidant.

Low levels of selenium in the soil are associated with increased cancer rates—and the opposite is true when the mineral is abundantly present. In Venezuela, the death rate from cancer of the large intestine is 3.06 per 100,000; in the United States it is 13.69 per 100,000. Venezuela has a high selenium content in the soil compared to the level in the United States.[1]

In one area of China, where the soil is extremely low in selenium, there is a rare form of heart disease called cardiomyopathy. Many children in the region have enlarged, weak hearts.

Selenium also boosts the immune system. Sources of this antioxidant include brewer's yeast, wheat germ, barley, oats, whole wheat, brown rice, butter, fish and lamb.

I recommend a daily multivitamin and mineral supplement that has 100 to 200 micrograms of chelated selenium.

COENZYME Q$_{10}$

An exciting antioxidant discovered in recent years is coenzyme Q$_{10}$, which is essential to the health of all our tissues. There are ten different coenzyme Qs, and 10 is considered the best.

Our body can produce coenzyme Q$_{10}$, but it usually doesn't make enough. The deficiencies are commonly seen in people with heart disease, periodontal disease (a form of gum disease), diabetes, ulcer disease, HIV and AIDS. For example, AIDS and heart disease patients have very low coenzyme Q$_{10}$ levels.

This nutrient is especially helpful for heart conditions, since it increases the pumping action and boosts the electrical system of the heart, helping to prevent arrhythmia. The recommended dose is 30 to 100 milligrams a day—and even higher doses in heart disease or heart failure cases. I personally take 100 milligrams a day.

Cholesterol-lowering drugs such as Mevacor, Pravachol, Zocor and Lipitor can actually block the synthesis of coenzyme Q$_{10}$ in the body. So when you're taking these drugs it is wise to supplement with this antioxidant.

Coenzyme Q$_{10}$ is found in sardines, spinach, peanuts and beef. Since we may not take in adequate amounts, I recommend that it be included in your multivitamin and mineral supplement.

ALPHA-LIPOIC ACID

For years alpha-lipoic acid, a natural antioxidant, has been used in Europe to treat alcoholic hepatitis and mushroom poisoning. It is also used in diabetic neuropathy. Over time, a diabetic may get to the point where he feels burning in his feet, legs or hands. Alpha-lipoic acid may prevent this sensation, so I recommend that every diabetic take this antioxidant daily.

It is also beneficial to protect the liver, to help detoxify the effects of medicine and for radiation sickness. It neutralizes free radicals in both the water-soluble and fat-soluble parts of the body.

An amazing aspect of alpha-lipoic acid is that it helps to recycle and extend the life span of vitamin C, glutathione, coenzyme Q_{10} and vitamin E. In other words, when you are taking alpha-lipoic acid and other antioxidants, it recycles them—so you use them over and over and over again. The best food source is red meat and liver. However, supplements are needed in order to obtain the needed doses, and again, I do not recommend that you eat liver. Choose lean, free-range red meat.

I recommend that you take 50 to 100 milligrams a day in your supplement—and more for disease states.

GRAPE SEED EXTRACT AND PINE BARK EXTRACT

You have probably read that French men have among the lowest incidence of heart disease and cancer. Many physicians attribute this to the fact that they drink red wine. Drinking an alcoholic beverage, however, is not necessary for the same benefit. The seed of the grape—not the grape itself—is one of the strongest antioxidants known to man.

Grape seed extract is twenty times more powerful than vitamin C and fifty times more powerful than vitamin E. In fact, of the twenty thousand or more bioflavonoids, this is the most potent.

A cousin to grape seed extract is pine bark extract, which is an extract from the bark of the French Maritime pine (found on the North Atlantic coasts of the United States, Canada and in Europe). Native Indians have used the bark of this tree for thousands of years, and it was only recently rediscovered by modern science.

I recommend that you start taking grape seed extract and/or pine bark extract. They are wonderful antioxidants to protect against cancer and heart disease and to guard the skin and organs from aging. You need about 50–100 milligrams a day—I personally take more.

A friend who is a chiropractor takes 200 milligrams of grape seed extract daily. At the age of forty he was having back pain every day from a bulging disk. Taking this antioxidant resulted in the pain's disappearance. Although there are no studies confirming this, I will continue both to take this supplement daily and recommend it to my patients.

EAT THOSE FRUITS AND VEGGIES!

MEDICAL RESEARCH HAS discovered that fruits and vegetables contain *phytonutrients*—super antioxidants that are formed in foods. Leading pharmaceutical companies are now working to extract these phytonutrients because of their potent medicinal effects in the prevention and treatment of cancer and other diseases.

The special foods we are about to discuss need to be eaten fresh. It makes little difference whether you juice, lightly steam, stir-fry or eat them raw. What is critically important, however, is that you eat these foods several times each week.

CABBAGE, BROCCOLI AND CAULIFLOWER

Cruciferous vegetables such as cabbage, brussel sprouts and broccoli contain several phytochemicals capable of helping the body handle cancer-causing estrogens. These phytochemicals include indole-3-carbinol (I3C), phenethyl isothiocyanate (PEITC), sulforaphane and diindolymethane (DIM). If you don't like these vegetables, you may take indole-3-carbinol in a dose of 500 milligrams two times a day. Or even better is DIM or Indolplex in a dose of 60 milligrams two times a day. Please see Appendix for ordering information.

Taking DIM, the most active cruciferous indole, as a supplement can restore and maintain a favorable balance of estrogen metabolites. DIM provides an innovative approach to reducing the risk of breast cancer and uterine cancer, thereby reducing the risks associated with estrogen replacement therapy. It has similar benefits for men, possibly serving as a basis for enhancing prostate health.

Unfortunately, most people eat these vegetables with polyunsaturated fats and margarine, which cause the lipid peroxidation we have discussed.

If you know someone with breast cancer, encourage them to eat cabbage every day—whether it is in the form of soup, juice, stir-fried or steamed.

"What about coleslaw?" you may ask. Yes, it's cabbage—but with mayonnaise. And remember, regular mayonnaise is your enemy because it is forming free radicals. You may use mayonnaise from the health food store that contains grape oil. If your cabbage is not organically grown, peel off the first layers to help avoid pesticides.

Some people substitute cabbage leaves for lettuce in their salads and flavor the taste by adding a little olive oil and vinegar.

Broccoli has disease-preventing phytonutrients called sulforaphanes and isothiocyanates. Broccoli also stimulates enzymes, which detoxify cancer-causing agents.

Carrots and tomatoes

Both carrots and tomatoes, mentioned earlier, have a natural antioxidant mixture of carotenoids, which are superior to beta carotene.

Lycopene is a strong phytonutrient found in tomatoes that can help prevent cancer of the prostate and colon. Cooked and processed tomatoes are higher in lycopene than raw tomatoes. The men in a Harvard study with the greatest protection against cancer consumed a minimum of 6.5 milligrams a day. If you dislike tomato-based foods, you can now buy lycopene capsules at the health food store.

GREEN TEA

The people of Japan have consumed green tea for thousands of years. It contains polyphenols, a phytonutrient found in greater amounts than any other tea. This antioxidant is nearly 200 times stronger than vitamin E and 500 times more potent than vitamin C as an antioxidant.

Green tea is very effective in preventing esophageal, stomach and lung cancer, even in smokers. Any smoker or ex-smoker should be drinking or taking capsules of green tea in order to prevent lung cancer. Many Americans today have reflux esophagitis, which can lead to a precancerous condition called Barrett's esophagus. Drinking green tea daily will help prevent cancer of the esophagus. You should drink at least one cup of sugar-free green tea three times a day; if you dislike the taste of the tea, take one 170-milligram capsule three times a day.

GARLIC AND ONIONS

Don't worry about garlic and onions keeping friends away. Be thankful they can distance you from disease. Research continues to show that those who eat a diet high in garlic and onions have less chance of developing stomach cancer. Garlic contains alliin, an active ingredient that helps slow the growth of tumors and inhibits the formation of esophageal, stomach and colon cancers.

Garlic has many medicinal uses. It helps prevent heart disease by lowering cholesterol and triglycerides, lowering blood pressure and decreasing the stickiness of platelets, which helps prevent blood clots. Garlic also has antiviral, antibacterial, antifungal and antiparasitic properties. Eating garlic regularly will also help reduce the risk of esphogeal, stomach and colon cancer. The usual dose of garlic is 500–600 milligrams three times a day.

BERRIES, GRAPES AND NUTS

Ellagic acid, a cancer-suppressing antioxidant, is found in berries, grapes and nuts. It helps to neutralize cancer and the toxins that cause cancer. These foods also protect against damage to our chromosomes. Ellagic acid also stimulates glutathione and other detoxification enzymes that inactivate toxins in the tissues.

Be sure you are not allergic to berries–especially strawberries. Try to buy organic grapes and berries to avoid the pesticides.

SOY

Many nutritionists believe that the phytonutrients in soy foods make soy the most powerful antioxidant.

Research shows that women consuming soy on a consistent basis in the United States have a much less incidence of developing cancer—especially cancer of the breast. I am convinced that both cabbage and soy are imperative for women to prevent breast cancer. They are also vital for men in the prevention of prostate cancer.

The potent phytonutrients in soy include protease inhibitors and plant estrogens such as genistein and diadzen, otherwise known as isoflavones. Genistein is the most powerful plant estrogen. Cancers are able to create new blood vessels; this is called angiogenesis. The genistein in soy is able to prevent the growth of new blood vessels in laboratory cultures.

The Japanese consume thirty to fifty times more soy than Americans. This may be the reason why the rates for breast cancer and prostate cancer are four times higher in the U.S. than in Japan.

It is interesting to note, however, that when Japanese men come to America and begin to eat Western food, their rate of prostate cancer elevates to that of Americans—which is high.

FIGHTING ON MANY FRONTS

ANTIOXIDANTS WORK SYNERGISTICALLY as a team—similar to a relay race.

The partially detoxified free radical is handed off to the next antioxidant in line until there are no more free radicals or antioxidants left. However, if there is not enough of a particular antioxidant in the chain, a buildup of free radicals can occur and cause toxicity and damage to the cells. That is why we need to make sure we have plenty of antioxidants, so that we can totally detoxify the free radicals.

You can't just take one antioxidant, such as vitamin C, and say, "I'm protected." All you're doing is protecting the water-soluble area of your body. But what about the fat-soluble areas, like the lipid membrane? We need full protection. I believe that a full complement of antioxidants offers the best protection, and taking a single antioxidant such as vitamin C in high doses may actually prove to be harmful. This, however, remains controversial.

Water-soluble antioxidants include vitamin C, pine bark extract, grape seed extract and most phytonutrients. "Water-soluble" means that it dissolves in water and moves freely in the bloodstream. Fat-soluble antioxidants can dissolve in fat and enter into the tissues. Remember that every cell has a fatty membrane, and only fat-soluble antioxidants are able to dissolve in fat. Therefore we need a mixture of fat-soluble and water-soluble antioxidants. Fat-soluble antioxidants include vitamin E, vitamin A, beta carotene and coenzyme Q_{10}. Alpha-lipoic acid is both water-soluble and fat-soluble.

An example of antioxidants working together is in the disease oral leukoplakia.

I'm sure you have observed baseball players chewing tobacco or dipping snuff. The "chew" is laying against their mucous membrane, and over the years even the most macho athlete may develop a condition called oral leukoplakia, a whitish plaque on their mucous membrane. If this is left untreated for over ten years, it usually progresses to mouth cancer (even if the individual stops dipping or chewing snuff).

Studies have shown that vitamin E will decrease the leukoplakia condition by as much as 50 percent. However, if vitamin E is added with beta carotene, the disease can be cured in as many as 75 percent of the cases.

I agree with nutritionists who have concluded that you need a combination of antioxidants in order for them to work the way they should. Remember, your fight against disease is waged on many fronts.

Don't go into battle only partially protected. You need it all—your shield, your sword and your helmet. Your body needs to be fortified with a combination of fruits, vegetables, vitamins, minerals and an armor of antioxidants.

DR. COLBERT'S CHECKLIST
FOR ANTIOXIDANTS

⋏ Take a quality multivitamin with a chelated mineral supplement.

⋏ Be sure to take zinc, copper and manganese, which the body uses to form the potent antioxidant SOD.

⋏ Take selenium in a chelated form—100 to 200 micrograms per day.

⋏ Take vitamin A—5,000 units a day.

⋏ Take vitamin C—at least 500 milligrams three times daily.

⋏ Take natural vitamin E—at least 400 units a day.

⋏ Take beta carotene—25,000 units a day (preferably from fresh carrots).

⋏ Take NAC—500 milligrams a day.

⋏ Take coenzyme Q_{10}—30 to 100 milligrams a day.

⋏ Take alpha-lipoic acid—50 to 100 milligrams a day.

⋏ Take grape seed extract or pine bark extract—at least 50 milligrams a day.

⋏ Eat cabbage, broccoli, cauliflower, carrots, tomatoes, berries, grapes, nuts, soy products, garlic and onions, and drink green tea—or take these in supplement form.

9

THE SEDUCTION OF
A SEDENTARY LIFE

W E'VE COME A long way from the time a man would begin
his day by cutting firewood, completing his chores at
home and then walking miles to work.

Today, the average forty-five-year-old man lives a "sedentary"
life. After a quick shower he sits at the breakfast table, then rides
in a comfortable car to his job—parking as close to the building as
possible. He takes an elevator to his office where he sits in an
executive chair until noon. That's when he gets back in his car and
heads for a local café or to the drive-through window of a fast-
food restaurant for a hamburger and fries to eat at his desk back at
the office. The rest of the afternoon he's secure in his chair—on
the phone, dictating or staring at a computer screen.

At day's end, he drives home, heads for the sofa and begins flicking through the television channels until his wife serves dinner—often delivered to the TV room. Then it's back to channel-surfing until the 11 o'clock news and bedtime.

How many steps has this man walked in the average day? What has he done to elevate his heart rate? Where is the exercise?

A similar saga can be written about working women. And what about the "soccer moms"? They spend their day driving the kids to activities, arriving home exhausted—but not from exercise.

DEGENERATION OF FITNESS

IF WE APPLIED a modern expression—"You've come a long way, baby"—to the issue of physical exercise in today's ultra-convenient lifestyle, we wouldn't be indicating a positive change—it would indicate a decline in fitness. And the decline just may be one of the factors that is killing Americans today!

Everywhere, because of a lack of intentional exertion, people are on the road to ruin—and don't even know it!

How "out of shape" are today's workers? In one community, the chief of police ruled that doughnut shops were "off limits" to his officers. That's where they were spending much of their time, and it showed in their waistline. I once treated a police officer who weighed over four hundred pounds. I could not imagine him tying his shoelaces, let alone chasing a suspect down the street.

Policemen, instead of walking their rounds, are now riding. It's also true of postmen. And firemen often become known for their fire-station cuisine at the expense of their exercise program.

THE DEGENERATION OF FITNESS

THE DECLINE IN fitness and physical exercise began long before the days mentioned in this chapter's opening paragraph. We only need to look at early history to understand why being fit is essential. The Bible, for example, is filled with accounts of people who were spiritually—and physically—strong.

Noah, who lived to be nine hundred fifty years old, must have been in excellent shape when, at the age of five hundred, he began to build the ark. He and his sons worked on the project for nearly one hundred years before the floods came. The ark was a huge undertaking. Its tonnage was equivalent to more than six hundred freight cars, which would form a train about four miles long. Historians note that until one hundred fifty years ago there was no ship in the world as large as the ark. That's what I call exercise!

Moses climbed Mount Sinai *twice* when God delivered His commandments to the children of Israel. (Mount Sinai could have been as high as 7,000 feet.) Then, at the age of one hundred twenty—after walking through the wilderness for decades—Moses climbed Mount Nebo. (From the top of Mount Nebo, a very high mountain, nearly all of Canaan could be seen. It was from the top of this high mountain that God gave Moses a glimpse of the Promised Land.)

Samson was endowed with incredible strength—so powerful that he once killed a thousand Philistines (Judg. 15:15). It's also recorded that when he was bound with ropes he broke them off like threads (Judg. 16:12).

David was physically strong. He was constantly on the move—from the mountains to the wilderness—engaged in battle after battle. He once killed a lion and a bear (1 Sam. 17:34–35).

Elijah, after his confrontation with the prophets of Baal on Mt. Carmel, received a message from Jezebel that he was about to be killed. He must have been in great condition, since the Bible records that he "fled for his life" (1 Kings 19:3). He went a day's journey through treacherous territory.

Jesus was a carpenter and knew what physical work entailed. He also walked nearly everywhere He went. The journey from Nazareth to Jerusalem, for example, is seventy-five miles. Once the Lord walked in the Judean wilderness for forty days—without food.

BENEFITS AND CONSEQUENCES

CHAPTER 28 OF Deuteronomy begins by listing the blessings that will come to those who obey the voice of the Lord. Then it presents the "curses" that will surely befall the disobedient. There are also consequences involved in the way we take care of our bodies.

There are wonderful primary benefits to a consistent exercise program: It increases the supply of oxygen to our tissues and cells, and it reconditions the heart. Oxygen is the breath of life, yet many are receiving an inadequate supply. In fact, a major cause of most degenerative diseases and early aging is simply lack of oxygen to the cells.

Recently, I had a patient who would not follow my recommendations regarding exercise and weight control. Finally, I gave her this stern message that many others need to hear. I asked, "Wouldn't you rather sow good seeds now through exercise than sit in a nursing home crippled with arthritis? Do you want to become so overweight that you don't have enough oxygen and smother on your own fat with sleep apnea?"

The facts are beyond dispute. The quality of your life in later years depends on whether or not you exercise—and on the care you take to exercise correctly. In this chapter we will see the benefits of good exercise, and we will learn how a lack of exercise—or incorrect or too much exercise—may be killing you.

A Well-Conditioned Heart

CARDIOVASCULAR DISEASE IS the most common cause of death in the United States today. It is prevalent because we clog our arteries by eating the wrong foods, and we do not *condition* the heart through proper physical activity.

When we exercise, the lungs take in more air and the heart grows stronger. As a result, the heart is able to pump more blood with fewer heartbeats.

Why is this so important? A well-conditioned heart has about sixty beats per minute, but an unconditioned heart has eighty beats—or more—per minute.

If you have ever owned a dog, perhaps you noticed the animal's rapid heartbeat. It's one of the reasons dogs live fewer years than humans. The heart of that little pet wears out from overuse.

Those twenty extra beats per minute of an unconditioned heart result in about one thousand two hundred extra beats per hour—nearly twenty-nine thousand extra beats a day and over ten million extra beats per year.

If you put excessive mileage on your car, it won't be long until the engine starts to sputter—and eventually fail. Just think of the consequences of adding ten million extra beats on your heart every year for twenty or thirty years. It's not a pretty picture.

There's another reason to condition your heart. *The slower the pulse, the greater the blood flow in the coronary arteries.*

Let me explain. Your heart and lungs are two organs that never take a break. They work when you're sleeping and when you're active—day and night, nonstop. So when your heart is constantly pounding away at eighty beats a minute, it's going to become tired and say, "I need more oxygen."

Your heart, the size of your fist, is supplied by two coronary arteries—right and left. The faster the heartbeat, the less blood (and oxygen) can flow through your coronary arteries. The opposite is also true. The slower the pulse, the greater the blood flow. Here's the most important fact of all. When the heart is beating, the blood can't flow in the coronary arteries—it only flows *between* beats, when the heart is relaxed.

Visualize this: The longer the pause from beat to beat, the more blood is being supplied to the coronary arteries, which nourish the heart. The well-conditioned heart has a much longer rest period, so that more blood can flow to the heart muscle—thus making a healthier heart. Exercise *enlarges* the coronary arteries, adding to the blood flow.

CHELATION THERAPY

There are about 170,000 heart-bypass surgeries per year in the United States at a cost of over two billion dollars. Yet many could have been prevented by practicing the principles found in this book.

If you (or someone you love) are a candidate for a bypass, look into the option of chelation therapy—a noninvasive method of removing toxic materials such as lead and cadmium. In this procedure, you receive an IV once or twice a week for about thirty to forty treatments. To find out more about this procedure or to find a physician in your area, call 1-800-LEADOUT.

NANOBACTX PRESCRIPTION

The tiniest, "nano"-sized organism known to man is the nanobacteria, called *Nanobacterium sanguineum,* which is a blood bacteria. They are from 20–200 nm in size and are described as the smallest known self-replicating organisms. Nanobacteria secrete a calcific coating around itself for protection, which creates problems when the organisms gather together and function as a unit or colony. We now understand that nanobacteria cause pathological calcification in heart disease, aortic and carotid plaque, coronary artery plaque and many other conditions.

There are laboratory tests that will reveal whether these *Nanobacterium sanguineum* antigens are involved in your heart problems. Once it is determined that you do indeed have a nanobacterial infection, it is recommended that you use NanobacTX, a compounded prescription medication. It is the only nanobiotic scientifically designed to safely remove the calcification from around the calcified nanobacteria, eliminating the bacteria. Additionally, NanobacTX is the only prescription treatment that may help to reverse coronary artery calcification. (For more information on screening tests for nanobacterial infections, visit Nanobac Labs at www.nanobaclabs.com or call 1-813-264-2241.)

EXERCISE

What's the best method of preventing arterial problems? Exercise. It can actually cause *collateral* arteries to form when the coronaries are becoming clogged with plaque. This creates a natural bypass around the plaque by building more blood vessels.

Recently I had a patient with an 80–90 percent blockage in his leg. After being on an aerobic exercise program for six months to a year, repeat studies found that he had formed a natural bypass around that plugged artery. That's what exercise can do!

But be sure that you have checked with your doctor before beginning any exercise program. Your heart is a muscle, and it must be conditioned gradually and consistently—like all your muscles—to reach its optimum peak performance. Don't try to run a five-mile marathon tomorrow if you have been a couch potato for the last five years.

ALL ABOUT AEROBICS

THE WORD *AEROBIC* means "with oxygen." It is a form of exercise that includes brisk walking, swimming, rowing, cycling, aerobic dancing and jogging. Aerobic exercise is something you can do at either a gentle or brisk pace that increases your heart rate.

The following example for a forty-year-old female will help you see how to determine your heart rate. Here's how to determine your training heart rate:

1. Subtract your age from 220.

2. Multiply that number by 65 percent, and then multiply that same number by 80 percent.

For example, if your age is 40, subtract that number from 220, and you have 180. Sixty-five percent of that is 117, and 80 percent of 180 is 144. So your heart rate needs to be elevated to between 117 and 144 to get the maximum aerobic response from exercise.

THIRTEEN BENEFITS

WHY SHOULD YOU add a daily workout to your schedule? Here are thirteen benefits of aerobic exercise.

1. IT MAY RAISE YOUR GOOD CHOLESTEROL—THE HDL.

You should have your cholesterol checked regularly. You'll notice the improvement when you are involved in regular aerobic exercise.

2. IT MAY LOWER YOUR BLOOD PRESSURE.

Do you realize that high blood pressure is one of the major risk factors for stroke and heart attack? About 20 percent of the population has high blood pressure—and the side effects of the medicines to lower it include fatigue and impotence. Aerobic exercise may lower the pressure without medication.

3. IT PREVENTS BLOOD CLOTS.

Daily vigorous exercise may increase the size of your arteries and vessels, thus lowering the risks of blood clots.

4. IT REDUCES THE DANGERS OF DIABETES.

Aerobic exercise improves the blood sugar control in non-insulin-dependent diabetics and decreases insulin requirements in insulin-dependent diabetics.

5. IT PROMOTES WEIGHT LOSS.

Approximately one out of three Americans is obese. That number is far too high. Obesity is a risk factor for high blood pressure, diabetes, arthritis and more.

6. IT HELPS TO RAISE THE METABOLIC RATE.

By increasing the muscle mass, exercise raises the body's basal metabolic rate. It is perhaps the safest method of accomplishing this goal.

7. IT MAY DECREASE YOUR APPETITE.

Aerobic activity may lower your craving for food. It also helps to keep your mind on physical conditioning rather than on hamburgers and French fries.

8. IT INCREASES PERSPIRATION.

Yet another advantage of exercise is that it increases perspiration, which is a vital method for the body to rid itself of waste products. Perspiration helps keep the skin clean and supple, and it also regulates the temperature of the body. Perspiration may not be fashionable, but it's healthy! We live in air-conditioned homes, work in air-conditioned offices, drive in air-conditioned cars, shop in air-conditioned malls and exercise in air-conditioned gyms. We wear antiperspirants to keep us from perspiring. Most Americans live a sedentary lifestyle that discourages perspiration. The result is a buildup of toxins in the bodies of most Americans—toxins that are clearly associated with a wide variety of degenerative diseases.

Don't be afraid to perspire when you exercise; it means you are healthy. I believe one of the reasons God created the summer was so that people can perspire out of their systems many of the poisons they accumulated during the fall, winter and spring seasons. The skin has been called "the third kidney" by some in the medical field because it is able to release so many toxins such as pesticides, solvents, heavy metals, urea and lactic acid from the body. Approximately 99 percent of perspiration is water; the remaining 1 percent is generally toxic waste. Brushing the skin with a loofah brush or any rough brush can help remove dried skin that accumulates on the epidermis. I recommend brushing dry skin prior to taking a shower. This brushing can help improve excretion of toxins by unclogging sweat pores.

Exercise not only eliminates toxins by increasing perspiration, as we have mentioned, but it also improves circulation to the skin, which brings nutrients to nourish the skin and remove cellular waste products. The nutrients to the skin help repair and rejuvenate the skin, usually causing a more youthful appearance.

9. IT TONES THE MUSCLES.

Aerobic exercise also improves muscle tone. It's the best cure for flabby, fleshy skin and muscles.

10. IT IMPROVES DIGESTION AND HELPS ELIMINATION FUNCTION.

Regular exercise increases the frequency of bowel movements and acts to stimulate the entire digestive system.

11. IT PROMOTES A MORE RESTFUL SLEEP.

A good workout reduces the "stress chemicals" in your body. As a result, you are relaxed and able to fall asleep sooner and to have a "deeper" rest. Try exercising late in the afternoon or early evening to release the tensions of everyday life.

12. IT REDUCES STRESS AND ANXIETY.

One researcher conducted an experiment with laboratory rats. He first subjected some rats to a program of stressors—shocking them with electrodes, shining bright lights and playing loud noises around the clock. At the end of one month, all the rats were dead from the stress.

He then took another group of rats and pretreated them with exercise on a treadmill. After a month of subjecting them to the same shocks, noises and lights, these rats were running around well and healthy.

Exercise helps relieve depression by elevating the endorphins. Endorphins are produced in the brain and act as an opiate by producing analgesia, which increases a sense of well-bring. The most active of these endorphin compounds are beta-endorphins—chemicals that make us feel good.

13. IT IMPROVES LYMPHATIC FLOW.

Another extremely important result of aerobic exercise is related to the lymphatic system, a system about which many people know very little. When the heart pumps blood, the blood follows two routes. One route is through the circulatory system of arteries and veins, and the other is through the lymphatic system. The lymphatic system has very small vessels that are present in all tissues and usually run alongside small veins and arteries. The small lymphatic vessels contain about fifteen liters of lymph fluid; in other words, there is about three times more lymph fluid in the body than actual blood.

As I explained in my book *What Would Jesus Eat?*, the lymphatic system is extremely important in eliminating toxins from the body, and also in maintaining the body's immune defenses. The lymphatic system includes the lymph nodes—every person has about six hundred lymph nodes that act as filters. The white blood cells in the lymph nodes scan the lymphatic fluid for bacteria, viruses, organic debris and other microbes. The white blood cells include macrophages, T-cells, B-cells and lymphocytes, which attack the viruses, fungi and bacteria. A very large part of the lymphatic system—at least 60 percent—is in the intestines, especially in the intestinal walls. When the lymphatic system is sluggish or blocked, white blood cells are slowed down or prevented from killing viruses, bacteria and other microbes. As a result, disease can more readily take root in the body.

Whereas blood serves primarily to feed oxygen and nutrients to the cells, the lymphatic fluid functions primarily to remove cellular waste. Lymphatic fluid circulates much more slowly than blood—in fact, it makes a full circuit through the body only once a day.

Lymphatic fluid is composed of approximately 50 percent plasma protein, and the lymphatic system is the major system for carrying blood plasma protein throughout the body. When the lymphatic system is impaired, protein—which is the essential building block for all cells—is unable to get to all of the body's cells efficiently. The plasma protein in the lymphatic system is about half of all the plasma protein circulated in the body. After circulating through the body in the lymphatic system, the plasma protein is passed back into the bloodstream. The lymphatics clear out lipoproteins, such as dangerous LDL (bad) cholesterol, and other toxic substances from circulation.

Lymphatic fluid enters the bloodstream or lymphatic system at the thoracic duct, which is in the left upper chest region. When the lymphatic fluid backs up or becomes stagnant due to infection or lack of exercise, the whole system can become toxic because of the failure of the lymphatics to dispose of cellular waste.

How does this flow of lymphatic fluid relate to exercise? The lymphatic system works differently than the blood circulatory system. The circulatory system depends upon the heart pumping blood. The lymphatic system, which actually flows upward against gravity in all areas of the body except the head and neck, depends upon muscle contractions for adequate flow. Muscle contractions actually push the fluid through the lymphatic channels. If activity level decreases, the flow of the lymphatic fluid is much more sluggish. Aerobic exercise can increase lymphatic flow threefold! That means three times the amount of cellular waste, foreign microbes, arterial plaque and LDL (bad) cholesterol is removed with adequate aerobic exercise.

A more rapid flow of lymphatic fluid also means that proteins are more readily recirculated into the bloodstream. When these proteins back up in the lymphatic system, they tend to attract water. The result is often swelling or edema in different tissues of the body.

Some of the best aerobic activities to stimulate lymphatic flow seem to be jumping rope and jumping on a mini-trampoline. If you are unable to exercise, an excellent alternative is the Chi Machine, which provides essential benefits that may help improve lymphatic drainage without placing stress on your heart and joints. Effective lymphatic drainage through exercise or the Chi Machine will help prevent disease. (See Appendix for ordering information.) Remember, a stagnant body breeds disease.

WHY WALK?

I'M CONVINCED THAT the best form of exercise is brisk walking—outside in the fresh air. It can give you three times the normal amount of oxygen.

One of my patients started walking briskly four times a week for thirty minutes, and after one year she had lost eighty pounds. "What about your diet?" I asked her.

"I didn't change my eating habits at all," she informed me.

Start walking! All you need is an inexpensive good pair of tennis shoes with ample arch support.

Be sure to walk at a pace that will condition your heart—your objective is to have a healthy heart that beats slower and becomes stronger.

At a seminar, someone asked, "Exactly how fast should I walk?"

I answered, "If you're unable to talk while walking briskly, slow down. However, if you can sing while walking, speed up." In other words, walk fast enough so that you can't sing, yet slow enough so that you can talk.

HOW MUCH EXERCISE?

REMEMBER: THE RIGHT amount of exercise is as important to observe as the fact that you exercise. There are dangers to too much exercise—just as there are dangers to too little exercise. An illustration from my own experience dramatically points out the danger of too much exercise.

Each year at the university I was attending, we were required to complete a three-mile race and a one-and-one-half-mile race at various times throughout the year. However, if your time was fast enough during the first race, you could earn an exemption from the later events.

During my third year I thought, *My schedule's too busy for all these races. I'll just break my record the first time.*

It was extremely hot on that day—about 98 degrees with almost 100 percent humidity. At the starting line I was totally focused, and I took off at breakneck speed.

Well, about fifty yards from the finish line my legs suddenly felt like rubber. I barely completed the race, and then collapsed on the ground. My face was contorted, and my heart was beating so fast I could hardly breathe.

"I've had a heat stroke," I told those who were hovering over me. "Quick. Get me some water!"

I was as hot as fire, and I had stopped sweating. They drenched me with a water hose—yet I was still not sweating. They rushed me to the hospital, and I told the emergency physicians, "Get an IV in each arm quick. I'm having a heat stroke."

By the time my wife, Mary, arrived, the IVs were in and the pores of my body began to act like thousands of little sprinklers—with water coming up out of each pore.

The condition was so severe that it destroyed the muscles in my legs—with muscle protein coming out in my urine for one month. My kidneys shut down, and I was confined to a wheelchair.

This was the toughest year of medical school, yet I was in the hospital and couldn't walk! I had a full recovery due to tremendous prayer, but pushing myself to the max was nearly a life-threatening mistake.

Your goal should be to maintain a thirty-minute aerobic exercise program at least four days a week. You say, "That's impossible. I'll be out of breath after five minutes."

Fine. Start slowly with five minutes a day, and increase the time and speed as you feel comfortable. It may take a month to reach your daily target.

The easiest way to exercise is to choose the same time every day and build it into your schedule. A workout before breakfast, lunch or dinner is great. Just don't exercise late at night, since you may be too charged up to sleep.

Avoid physical exertion immediately after a meal. Why? Exercise will pull the blood from your stomach and intestines (where it's needed to help digestion) to your muscles. You are likely to start belching and to have heartburn and other digestive problems. Exercise before you eat or two hours after you eat.

When your workout is complete, you should feel energized and refreshed—not exhausted. If you are feeling drained, you may have gone through the routine too quickly. Slow down! Do it properly and reap the rewards.

To determine the proper time for exercise, ask yourself, "When do I want the greatest charge?" If you exercise before breakfast, you're empowered for the morning. If you choose lunchtime, you're charged for the afternoon.

OUT OF TIME?

YOU MAY SAY, "I don't have time for exercise! What can I do?"

Until you decide to set your alarm clock thirty minutes earlier, here are three strategies worth adopting:

- Drive your car to the far end of the parking lot and walk to your office.
- Use the stairs, not the elevator.
- Bring your lunch to work, and use the extra time to take a walk.

If you become tired during the day and need to wake up in a hurry, it's easy. Stand up tall, take a deep breath through your nose and exhale through your mouth. Try it every hour. By pumping oxygen into your system, you're going to have more mental clarity and feel renewed.

WORKING WITH WEIGHTS

THE MOST EFFECTIVE strength-building exercise is weight training. While aerobics are great for the heart and lungs, weight-bearing exercises and calisthenics will help build strong bones and muscles.

Find a weight that you can lift for at least eight, but not more than twelve, repetitions. You'll be training at about 60 percent of your maximum ability and will prevent injury and excessive free radicals.

Perform each repetition slowly using good control. I highly recommend that your initial sessions be with a certified personal trainer who knows the correct form and technique. That person can get you started on the right program. It's also helpful—and safer—to lift weights with a friend.

CALISTHENICS

You can simply use your own body weight to build muscles—no other equipment is needed. In addition to walking, calisthenics include push-ups, pull-ups, sit-ups, lunges, calf-raises and dozens more exercises.

Both weight training and calisthenics are effective in the prevention of osteoporosis—the thinning of the bones that affects about twenty-five million Americans. It occurs mainly in women past the age of fifty, but it can also affect men. A person with the condition may start shrinking in size—or develop a hump on their back.

From age thirty on, everyone needs to exercise either with weights or calisthenics to keep bones strong.

Remember, low-intensity workouts are not harmful. It's the *lack* of exercise that invites disease—and worse.

THE FLEXIBILITY FACTOR

EVERY GOOD EXERCISE session needs to begin with a warmup. This activity involves some serious stretching, which prepares your body for a more strenuous workout.

The person suffering from arthritis, however, should focus on flexibility and stretching. You want to put your joints through a full range of motion. Those with arthritis need to perform lighter workouts in aerobics, weightlifting and calisthenics. You should always stretch prior to exercising. As joint pain and swelling diminish, you can gradually increase the intensity of the workouts.

Stretching prevents injuries, and it should precede every aerobic and strength-building workout. Here are four tips:

- Inhale deeply before the stretch.
- Exhale during the stretch.
- Perform all stretching exercises slowly and without bouncing.
- Never stretch so much that it begins to hurt.

RELIEVING BACK PAIN

BACK PAIN WILL affect over 80 percent of Americans at some point in their life. That's why we have so many chiropractors and orthopedic surgeons.

Without question, flexibility exercises and abdominal strengthening routines are most important for a healthy back. Follow these tips for your back pain relief:

212

- Adequate daily water intake (at least two quarts daily) is essential for healthy disks of the back and for adequate synovial fluid to keep the joints lubricated.

- To avoid strain on your lower back, always lift heavy objects by bending your knees, not your waist.

- Maintain good posture.

- Avoid excessive jarring exercises—including running.

I have a friend who is a dermatologist and plastic surgeon, and he loves to run marathons. However, he developed serious back problems from disks that were wearing out and from arthritis of the back.

If you have similar back problems, avoid the "jarring" motion of running on a hard surface. Switch to cycling, swimming, brisk walking or other low-intensity exercises. They're better than running or jogging because they condition our hearts without damaging or destroying our joints or disks.

High-intensity activity—where you're huffing and puffing—can result in injury to muscles, tendons, joints or ligaments and can form many more free radicals, which may lead to cataracts, heart attacks, cancer, accelerated aging and decreased immune function. That's why you need an exercise that works *with* your body, not against it. I also strongly recommend taking antioxidants both before and after exercising.

THE DANGERS OF INACTIVITY

WE'VE TALKED ABOUT the benefits of planned physical exertion, but what about the "curses" that result from inactivity? Here are eight:

1. Depression and sluggishness
2. Bowels that become constipated
3. Soft and flabby muscles
4. Compromised digestion resulting in heartburn and indigestion
5. Poor memory retention and slowed reaction time
6. Decreased lung capacity
7. Increased heart rate, which may lead eventually to cardiovascular disease
8. Tissues and cells that receive inadequate oxygen, inviting cancer-causing conditions

People who don't exercise slowly decay from the inside out. Do you know what happens to a car that is parked in the driveway and never driven? The paint begins to fade, the engine locks up and the body begins to rust.

A good low-intensity exercise regimen is a maintenance program that will keep your body under warranty. It's how you can help to ensure that every working part functions properly—your heart, lungs, kidneys, blood vessels and much more.

Listen to your body—it will clearly speak to you. Don't ignore the message. Make a concerted effort today to renew your lease on life through daily exercise. Don't fall into the seductive trap of a sedentary life.

DR. COLBERT'S CHECKLIST
FOR EXERCISE AND OXYGEN

⋏ Exercise increases the supply of oxygen to your tissues and cells and conditions the heart.

⋏ A lower heartbeat may extend life.

⋏ Walk briskly in fresh, clean air at least thirty minutes four times a week.

⋏ Aerobic exercise may raise good cholesterol, lower blood pressure and reduce stress.

⋏ Weight training and calisthenics are effective for prevention of osteoporosis.

⋏ Stretching and flexibility training are needed for those suffering from arthritis and back pain.

⋏ Avoid high-intensity physical activity unless medically cleared by a medical doctor.

10

The Perils of Personal Care and Household Products

E very morning you wake up, shut off the alarm and begin applying, spraying, brushing and patting from ten to thirty products on your body—all of which may contain chemicals that might be slowly killing you!

We are being bombarded from every side with toxins—often from sources we never consider. Do you actually know the ingredients in your hair conditioner, makeup, deodorant, perfumes, colognes, hair sprays and hand sanitizers?

The perils of personal products can silently undermine the safety of your home. Without your knowledge, poisons and cancer-causing substances can be absorbed slowly over time through your skin and lungs, and they can accumulate in your

216

body. Some personal and home products are made from some of the most toxic ingredients in existence. You can eat right, exercise, take supplements and do everything you know to live healthy, and still be filling your body and the bodies of your loved ones with dangerous toxins. What you don't know about the products you use may be killing you and your family. This chapter will provide powerful insight for you and help you to create a healthy, wholesome and safe environment for yourself and your family.

Personal care products and common household chemicals often contain an alphabet soup of chemicals and solvents. We are rubbing chemicals on our faces, applying them to our skin, spraying them on our hair, using them to wash our hands and clothes and cleaning our homes with them.

What is the harm? We are becoming toxic. Over time, the solvents found in personal care products and household products may collect in our central nervous systems, in our tissues and in our organs. Products that contain petroleum derivatives have properties that can damage our cardiovascular systems. They also have the potential to cause cancer.

You may think, *What on earth can I do? Are you telling me that even my deodorant, hair spray and cosmetics contain toxins?* That's right. And these accumulate in your body over time.

There are things that you can do to eliminate these toxins from your home and body. Start by using the following information to help you understand the problem and find solutions. You can radically change this situation by making better choices about personal care products and household chemicals that you use.

Take a close look at each of the products on the following pages. I have provided a brief overview of the product's potential dangers, recommended the safest brands to use and suggested healthier natural products or chemical-free solutions. Many of these products—and others—are explained in more detail in *The Safe Shopper's Bible,* a guide to nontoxic household products, cosmetics and food for consumers, by David Steinman and Samuel S. Epstein, M.D.

PERSONAL CARE PRODUCTS

COSMETICS AND PERSONAL care products have been around since civilization began, and it's doubtful that we would ever want to give up the primping and pampering of our bodies that personal care products and makeup provide. But for most of history, personal care products were made of natural ingredients. Today this is increasingly less so. The products that feel so good to our skin and look and smell so good on our faces and bodies often contain chemicals and dyes that we should be warned about.

You probably know someone who is taking a medication that is applied through the skin. This method is used for administering medicine for hormone replacement for both men and women, and also, a patch is used to treat high blood pressure. Skin patches can also be purchased over the counter to help smokers stop smoking. Although the body takes substances in through the skin in a much slower way, what you apply on your skin will eventually make its way into your body.

So why is it that most of us apply many personal products to our skin throughout the day but never consider that these products will end up in our organs and tissues throughout our bodies? They most certainly do.

Like most of us, you probably use your favorite personal products with the complete assurance that the federal government carefully tests and screens each one and would never permit products with dangerous or toxic ingredients to reach the supermarket, drug store and department store shelves. Sadly, your confidence in government screening to protect you may be naïve. The Federal Food, Drug and Cosmetic Act (FFDCA) does not require premarket testing, review or approval for cosmetics. In addition, the Food and Drug Administration (FDA) will pursue enforcement action for problem cosmetics only *after* they are on the shelves.[1]

This means that it's up to you to understand what you are purchasing and to make wise, healthy choices regarding the personal products that you and your family will use.

The cosmetic industry may not tell you that some of the ingredients used in its products are hazardous to your health. Become informed about the possibility of allergy-producing and cancer-causing substances in your personal products—your life may depend on it.

TAKE A CLOSE LOOK AT YOUR TOOTHPASTE.

Do your children swallow toothpaste as they're brushing their teeth? Toothpaste can be highly toxic and can cause poisoning. So, be very careful. Most people never read the back label of their toothpaste, which usually issues a warning.

> Warning: As with all fluoride toothpastes, keep out of reach of children under 6 years of age. If an amount considerably larger than used for brushing is swallowed, seek professional assistance or contact a poison control center immediately.

Be sure and rinse your mouth out well after brushing your teeth; make sure you children do the same. I recommend rinsing the mouth out three times if using regular toothpaste. There are natural, alternative brands.

Some alternative natural choices: Beehive Botanicals Propolis Toothpaste, Nature's Gate toothpastes, Tom's of Maine toothpastes (nonfluoride), as well as many more.

MOUTHWASH

Mouthwashes made of 25 percent or more alcohol have been found to increase your risk of cancer.[2]

A survey of 866 patients with oral or pharyngeal cancers and 1,249 people without the disease showed that regular use of mouthwash may contribute to increased risk of cancers of the lips, tongue, mouth and throat.[3]

Never let your children swallow mouthwash—it can be fatal. A petition to bring attention to the danger of children using alcohol-containing mouthwashes has been filed with the Consumer Product Safety Commission by attorney generals of twenty-seven states and several medical and health organizations, including the American Academy of Pediatrics.[4] Those who oppose the sales of high-alcohol content mouthwashes argue that 10,000 children under the age of six have been poisoned by these mouthwashes in the past five years. Mouthwashes with large amounts of alcohol can cause seizures, brain damage and comas in small children, and drinking 5 ounces can be fatal.[5]

If you are in the habit of buying and using mouthwash, and especially if you allow your small children to use it, check the labels carefully before choosing a brand. Never buy brands that contain high amounts of alcohol. Avoid brands containing saccharin and blue, green or yellow dyes.[6]

Some alternative natural choices: Desert Essence, Logona Cistacea Oral Spray, Tom's Cinnamint Mouthwash.

THE CONCERN ABOUT SHAMPOOS

If you are like most of us, you've never even read the warning label on the back of your shampoo bottle. I encourage you to read it. What chemicals does it contain?

Your skin—even the skin on your scalp—is an organ that is able to absorb chemicals. What you put on your skin over time will end up in your body. If you don't believe me, try rubbing raw garlic on the bottom of your foot. Within minutes you will taste it in your mouth. Why not try it? It will certainly bring home the point I'm making. Be sure you know what you are putting on your body's largest organ.

Use the mildest, highest quality shampoos you can buy. Look for brands containing the following gentle cleansers:

- Amphoteric (-2, -6 and -20)
- Cocamide derivatives
- Lauramide (diethanolamide or monoethanolamide)
- Polysorbate (20 or 40)
- Sodium lauraminopropionate
- Sorbitan derivatives
- Stearamide derivatives

Avoid products with DEA and sodium lauryl sulphate.

Some alternative natural choices: There are many natural shampoos available, both in mainline department stores or in health food stores. Recommendations include Bindi Hair Wash, Desert Essence Tea Tree Oil Shampoo, Earth Preserve Shampoo (all scents; JC Penney), Faith in Nature shampoos and Ivory shampoos.

HARMFUL HAIR-COLORING PRODUCTS

Do you color your hair? The chemicals in hair dyes can be very dangerous, especially if you use the darker colors. Using them for years can increase your risk of certain cancers.

The use of permanent and semipermanent hair dyes is associated with significantly increased risk of non-Hodgkin's lymphoma, multiple myeloma, leukemia and Hodgkin's disease as well as possibly breast cancer. Women who use black, brown/brunette and red hair dyes have a greater risk than women who use lighter color dyes.[7]

Never use any product with the following disclaimer on the package:

> Caution: This product contains ingredients that may cause skin irritation on certain individuals. A preliminary test according to accompanying directions should first be made. This product must not be used for dyeing the eyelashes or eyebrows; to do so may cause blindness.[8]

Other cautions include:

· Flood scalp thoroughly with water after use.
· Use a technique that involves minimum contact between the dye and scalp (such as plastic caps with holes to pull hair through). Tipping, streaking or painting involves less contact.[9]

I also recommend:

· Never use a product that lists a phenylenediamine compound on its label.
· Bleaches are much safer than dyes.
· Put off using hair dyes as long as possible.

Some alternative natural choices: You can find some very acceptable all-natural hair coloring products. One line that is becoming widely popular is Igora Botanic from Schwarzkopf.

These plant-based hair colors are composed of materials found in nature such as indigo, chamomile, walnut, logwood, cochineal and guar gum. The line offers eight shades. For more information, call (800) 234-4672. Several other brands from Logona and Rainbow Research are also available.[10]

Interestingly, when I put some of my white- or gray-haired patients through a program of detoxification, get them taking a good multimineral supplement and a good hormonal program, their original hair color may actually return. One patient was seventy-five years old, with really gray hair. His hair actually started turning black again. Everyone thought he started dyeing it. But he did not; he simply started giving his body what it needed.

THE HARM OF HAIR SPRAYS AND STYLING PREPARATIONS

Avoid using aerosols! Aerosol particles are easily breathed in and are so fine that they penetrate to the deepest parts of the lungs, where they are transferred, like oxygen, into the bloodstream.

If you are in the habit of using an aerosol spray, my advice is to consider other alternatives. Have you ever noticed a ceiling fan near a bathroom where aerosol hair spray was used? It gets covered with a layer of sticky, dirty, greasy film. If that's what it does to a fan located several feet from your head, what do you think it does to your lungs when you spray it inches away from your mouth? Everything in that hair spray enters your lungs. Some hair sprays contain dyes and many other chemicals that are known to cause cancer.

Although pumps are better than aerosols, they still can cause chemicals to become airborne where you can breathe them in. Use pumps in well-ventilated areas. Better yet, try using hair-setting lotions instead.

Some recommended choices include Alberto VO5 with Cholesterol Damaged Hair Treatment, Aloegen hair products, Giovanni hair products and White Rain hair products.

Some alternative natural choices: Aubrey hair products use natural products such as ginkgo leaf, ginseng root and chamomile; they are excellent choices. Naturade products offer nonalcohol spray with jojoba. Check in your health food store to find other healthy choices.

THE MIRE OF MAKEUP

Makeup can cause skin irritations and acne. If you are experiencing acne, beware of the following acne-causing ingredients:

- Butyl stearate
- Cocoa butter
- Corn oil
- Isopropyl myristate
- Lauryl alcohol
- Linseed oil
- Margarine
- Methyl oleate
- Mineral oil
- Oleic acid
- Olive oil
- Peanut oil
- Petrolatum
- Safflower
- Sesame oil
- Stearic acid

Recommendations for foundations include Clinique Pore-Minimizer Makeup, Cover Girl Clarifying Makeup, Max Factor New Definition Makeup and Max Factor Pan-Stik Ultra Creamy Makeup.

Some alternative natural choices: Dr. Hauschka products and Physician's Formula Le Velvet Film Makeup are healthy choices. Check regularly with your health food store for new natural alternatives.

THE PROBLEM WITH ANTIPERSPIRANTS AND DEODORANTS

For the record: An antiperspirant stops you from perspiring, and a deodorant masks odor. Since antiperspirants contain aluminum and zirconium or their derivatives, I would strongly encourage you to stop using them. Aluminum has been linked to Alzheimer's disease.[11] So check the label and avoid products that contain aluminum and aluminum compounds.

Here is a list of problem chemicals found in antiperspirants:

- Aluminum chloride
- Aluminum chlorohydrate
- Aluminum phenolsulfate
- Aluminum sulfate
- Zinc phenolsulfonate
- Zirconium chlorohydrate
- Zirconyl chloride

In addition, deodorants may contain the chemical triclosan, which has been found to cause liver damage in laboratory rats.[12] Although the FDA has determined that it is safe, it has also warned of potential hazards for long-term use.[13] Many of the dyes and other chemicals contained in antiperspirants and deodorants are known carcinogens. My advice is to use the deodorant brands that contain talc. It causes no health risk when applied with the roll-on or solid varieties.

In addition, here's a list of safer choices: Ban Roll-On (Ocean Breeze and Unscented), Degree (roll-on and solid, Powder Fresh, Regular, Shower Clean and Unscented), Lady Speed Stick (no dyes or fragrance), Secret Roll-ons (Fresh, Regular, Sporty, Clean and Spring Breeze) or Sure Solid (Desert Spice, Outdoor Fresh, Powder Dry and Regular).

Some alternative natural choices: CamoCare deodorant, Home Health Roll-on Deodorant, Jason brand products, Logona deodorants, Nature De France deodorants, Tom's of Maine deodorants.

HARMFUL HOUSEHOLD PRODUCTS

YOU PROBABLY USE about ten to forty different household products both in your home and yard in an effort to create a clean, sanitary, safe environment for your family. What you may not realize is that the products you are using to make your home and lawn safe may be polluting your home environment with chemicals that are quietly harming you and your family!

More than seventy thousand chemical compounds are commercially produced. Many of these chemicals can accumulate in your body, and some can cause cancer. Others have not been adequately tested.[14]

Your home should be a safe place, not a toxic environment. The cleaning agents and household products in the next several pages will help you to reclaim a safe environment for both you and your family. Although I will not be able to list all of the many products you and your family may use, I will attempt to highlight some of the most significant dangers. I trust you will discover how important it is to search the labels and learn about what you don't know that might be harming you and your family.

THE PERILS OF ALL-PURPOSE CLEANERS

Many all-purpose cleaners in themselves are not generally dangerous. But what can be dangerous is how you use them. Do you mix chlorine cleaners with ammonia-based products? If you do, you could be creating dangerous, cancer-causing poisons. Never mix cleaners without carefully reading labels.

I encourage you to wear rubber gloves whenever you use any cleaning products. This will keep chemicals away from your skin so they are not absorbed into your body. In addition, make sure you use cleaning agents in well-ventilated areas. Strong fumes are not good for your lungs.

These simple precautions can go a long way in making the job of housecleaning safer for you. In addition, here is a list of some safe products you may want to try if you don't use them already: Mr. Clean products, SOS, Kitchen Safe, and Spic and Span liquid and detergent.

Some alternative natural choices: Many brands are widely available at both supermarkets and health food stores. Recommended natural products include Aubrey products, EarthRite cleaners and Naturally Yours degreaser and soap.

There are also many inexpensive ways of making your own all-purpose cleaners.

- A disinfectant cleaner can be made with a mixture of 1 teaspoon borax, 2 tablespoons distilled white vinegar, ¼ cup liquid soap and 2 cups hot water in a refillable spray bottle.

- A stronger all-around household cleaner can be made with liquid soap and trisodium phosphate (TSP). Again, use a refillable spray bottle. Mix 1 teaspoon liquid soap, 1 teaspoon TSP, 1 teaspoon borax, 1 teaspoon distilled white vinegar and 1 quart warm or hot water. This formula is effective against both grease and mildew. [15]

THE DANGER OF DISHWASHING LIQUIDS

It's best to use a dishwasher and stop washing dishes by hand. If you do still wash your dishes by hand, be sure to wear rubber or vinyl gloves. They will protect your skin from any harmful dyes and chemicals that dishwashing liquids may contain. In addition, some dishwashing liquids are petroleum based and contain harsh detergents. These should be avoided.

Some alternative natural choices: Supermarkets usually carry many good brands that contain neither fragrances nor dyes. Some recommended choices include Biofa Natural Dishwashing Liquid, EarthRite products, Simmons Pure Soaps and Tropical Soap Company Sirena Coconut Oil Bar Soaps.[16]

DEALING WITH LAUNDRY
DETERGENTS AND SOAPS

The gentlest brands of detergents are those made with vegetable-based detergents instead of harsher petroleum-based detergents. In addition, some detergents contain dangerous chemicals like triclosan.

Triclosan is a favorite antibacterial chemical used in detergents, dishwashing liquids, soaps, deodorants, cosmetics, lotions, creams and even toothpaste. The EPA registers triclosan as a pesticide. It is a chlorinated aromatic, similar in molecular structure and chemical formulation to some of the most toxic chemicals on earth: dioxins, PCBs and Agent Orange.[17]

Avoid eye contact with laundry detergents, and store them in a childproof area. Recommended choices include All, Cheer Free (both are perfume- and dye-free), Ivory Snow Soap Granules, Winter White Laundry Detergent Powder and Woolite Cold-Water Wash.

Some alternative natural choices: Use petroleum-free brands. These include EarthRite products, Naturally Yours Detergents, Shaklee products and Amway products.[18]

FINDING BETTER PAINT
AND RELATED PRODUCTS

Those who work with paint every day get cancer more often than the rest of us do. Painters are at risk for getting a wide range of cancers, including cancers of the esophagus, stomach and bladder—about 20 percent over the national average—and consistent excess of lung cancers—40 percent over the national average. Both oil-based and latex paints are neurotoxic because of the solvents they contain. Although it is commonly believed that new latex paints are lead-free, they may contain up to 0.06 percent lead, a neurotoxin.[19]

It is important to follow safety guidelines when using any paint product. These safety tips include:

- Provide adequate ventilation.
- Wear a respirator for all painting.
- Extinguish pilot lights when painting indoors. Most solvents are highly flammable.
- Do not leave paint containers open.
- Keep paints in their original containers.
- Use a sealing product such as Pace Chem Industries' Crystal Aire Acrylic Clear Finish to prevent paint fumes that might be emitted for days to months after paint is applied.
- Oil-based paints should never be used indoors due to the possibility of severe respiratory irritation.

Recommended choices include Glidden Spred 2000 Flat Wall Paint and Miller Paint Company products.

Some alternative natural choices: Auro Organics products and Biofa Natural products.[20]

THE PERIL OF PESTICIDES

SOME OF THE most dangerous environmental poisons may be found right in your backyard, or worse, under your kitchen sink!

A highly increased risk for leukemia exists for infants born immediately after the parents spray their home with pesticides. Pesticides are also suspect in the rising incidence of brain cancer in children.[21] No-pest strips, pesticides to control termites, flea collars on pets, diazinon in the garden, pesticide bombs in the home and herbicides used to control weeds are associated with child-hood cancer.[22] The active ingredient in many of these products is dichlorvos (DDVP), which is carcinogenic.[23]

Concerned Oregon residents have formed a coalition to demand open access to all information about pesticides that affect their environment.[24] All of us need to become informed regarding the dangers of pesticides in our homes and environments.

The following pesticides are known cancer-causers and should never be used:[25]

- Acephate
- Atrazine
- Benomyl
- Chlorothalonil
- 2,4-D
- DDVP

- Dacthal (DCPA)
- Isoxaben
- Maneb
- Permethrin
- Pronamide

The use of pesticides poses extreme hazards—except for some of the botanically derived pesticides. I strongly recommend against the use of any pesticides in the home and garden other than natural pyrethrum or pyrethrin extracts, fatty acid soaps and other natural biological and physical pesticides.

If you must use pesticides, spray them outside of your house, not inside. Follow these safety tips:

- Always read the labels and follow the directions to the letter.

- Don't use products for pests that are not indicated on the label, and don't use more pesticide than directed on the label.

- Use protective measures when handling pesticides, such as wearing rubber gloves, long pants and a long-sleeve shirt. Change your clothes, and shower immediately after applying pesticides.

- Remove children, toys and pets from areas in which pesticides are being applied.

- Don't spray outside on windy or rainy days. Be careful that pesticides cannot run into your pool, vegetable garden or your neighbor's yard.

- Remove and cover food before applying pesticides.

- Don't purchase more pesticides than you need for a single application.

- Keep the telephone number of your poison control center near your phone.

- In case of an emergency, determine what the individual was exposed to and what part of the body was exposed. Have the product with you when you arrive at the hospital.[26]

Better yet, try to use only safe products and safer solutions.

Some alternative natural choices:

- Ants and cockroaches—Take away their food. Put garbage in sealed metal containers with tight covers and keep cans outside. Wash food preparation and serving areas immediately following use. Clean storage, shelves and drawers. Fix all leaks. Keep areas under sinks and basins clean and dry.

- Garden pests—Use yellow sticky traps, available from most garden shops. Pyrethrins and fatty acid soaps work well when sprayed on infested plants. Use oil sprays without copper additives. Use good insects to destroy bad insects, such as lacewing larvae to destroy aphids, mites and whiteflies.

• Lawn care—Release natural predators such as praying mantises and beneficial nematodes. Drain, dry out and de-thatch wet, thatchy, overfertilized lawns. Mow often, and mow high. Do not rake; leave clippings on the lawn to act as a natural fertilizer and mulch.

Safe home and garden pesticides include the following:

• Black Flag Roach Ender Roach Control System
• Enforcer Roach Rid
• Perma Proof insect control products
• Safer insect control products
• Diphenamid

INSECT REPELLENTS

Insect repellents are also of great concern—especially to parents. The Environmental Protection Agency (EPA) encourages consumers to use nonchemical means of repelling mosquitoes whenever possible, such as screens, netting, long sleeves and slacks.[27]

Remember that what you apply on your skin will be absorbed into your body. It's best to never use chemical insect repellents to get rid of pesky mosquitoes. Look for natural methods instead. Your local health food store may be able to help. Soaps and lotions are available that are far less dangerous.

However, if you must use insect repellents, use them sparingly and with extreme caution. Follow these safety tips.

- Repellents should be applied only to exposed skin and/or clothing (as directed on the product label). Do not use under clothing.

- Never use repellents over cuts, wounds or irritated skin.

- Don't apply repellents to eyes and mouth, and use sparingly around ears. Do not spray directly onto your face.

- Do not allow children to handle these products.

- Do not spray in enclosed areas. Avoid breathing a repellent spray.

- Do not use near food.

- After returning indoors, wash treated skin with soap and water or shower.

- Wash clothing before you wear it again.

If you suspect that you or your child are reacting to an insect repellent, discontinue use, wash treated skin and call your local poison control center. Take the repellent with you to the doctor.[28]

Some alternative natural choices: Wear long sleeves and long pants, and use screens and netting. Look for soaps and natural products at your local health food store.

Ridding yourself of a few minutes of pesky discomfort is not worth subjecting yourself or your children to dangerous poisons. Our ancestors lived and thrived for centuries without the use of such products. Providing a safe environment for our families' health is one of the most important things we can do.

So, whenever you need a strong product to meet a daily need, use this rule of thumb: Find a natural solution first. If that doesn't work, find the safest products on the market and use them sparingly. Your family's health is well worth it!

CONCLUSION

A SAFE, HEALTHY home is a gift and a powerful haven of blessed refuge from the battles of daily life. To consider that, without your knowing it, poisonous, cancer-causing substances have been polluting that haven and attacking you and your family is offensive. I trust that the knowledge and insight provided in this chapter will prove a powerful weapon against the subtle onslaught of common toxins that pollute your environment. It is my desire that, armed with knowledge and practical advice, you can reclaim the healthful environment of your home, and that you and your family will live long, healthy lives, free from the destructive diseases that environmental pollutants can bring.

DR. COLBERT'S CHECKLIST FOR PERILS OF PERSONAL PRODUCTS

⋏ Do not swallow your toothpaste.

⋏ Be sure to buy the mildest shampoo.

⋏ Try purchasing safer natural hair dyes.

⋏ Do not mix chlorine cleaners or bleach with ammonia.

⋏ Provide adequate ventilation when painting.

⋏ Keep paints in their original containers.

⋏ Do not spray pesticides inside the home.

⋏ Use natural, safe methods of ridding your home of insects.

CONCLUSION

Y OU CAN ALMOST hear the sadness in God's voice when He
said, "My people are destroyed for lack of knowledge" (Hos.
4:6, KJV). In other words, God was saying, "What My people don't
know is killing them!" God never intended for you to suffer need-
lessly from painful diseases and physical degeneration. That is the
reason I've sought to inform you through the pages of this book.

Over the past several years I have traveled and met with some of
the greatest health and nutrition specialists around the world. As
I've met with each doctor or nutritionist, I have attempted to
glean the most powerful, up-to-date information about health and
natural medicine to provide to you.

So now you know—you are no longer ignorant or uninformed

of the many factors that may be harming your health.

Good health is a wonderful gift. But sadly, few individuals realize the blessing of that gift until it is too late. Take a minute to reexamine your own habits and personal health choices. Are you building a pathway of future good health by making careful and wise decisions today? Your physical, emotional and spiritual future is in your own hands. So please, never take today's good health for granted. For what you now know *can* save your life!

—Don Colbert, M.D.

APPENDIX

RECOMMENDED SOURCES AND ORGANIZATIONS

THE ALKALIZER WATER SYSTEM AND THE ALKALIZER WATER FILTER

E-mail: info@alkalizer.com

Fax: (407) 876-6893

DBS, Inc. has extended a special offer to readers of Dr. Colbert's publications. Please provide Dr. Colbert's special code number DC7007 to receive $100 dollars off the cost of each unit you purchase.

CHI MACHINE

Toll free: (888) 779-7177

Web site: www.chinow.com/divinehealth

You may also visit Dr. Colbert's Web site at www.drcolbert.com, click Preferred Products and click the link for the Chi Machine.

238

INTERNATIONAL COLLEGE OF INTEGRATIVE MEDICINE
Formerly Great Lakes College of Clinical Medicine (GLCCM)
Toll free: (866) 464-5226
Web site: www.glccm.org/icimed

DIVINE HEALTH NUTRITIONAL PRODUCTS
Web site: www.drcolbert.com
Order Divine Health Buffered Vitamin C, Divine Health Milk Thistle, Divine Health Elite Antioxidants and all of Dr. Colbert's other fine products.

BIO HYDRATION RESEARCH LAB, INC.
Web site: www.hydrateforlife.com for more information on Penta water

WELLNESS SHOWER FILTERS
Toll free: (888) 611-0112

AMERICAN COLLEGE FOR ADVANCEMENT IN MEDICINE (ACAM)
Toll free: (800) 532-3688
Web site: www.acam.org

ALKALIZER DROPS BY CILI MINERALS
Phone: (337) 993-9660

Q.C.A. SPAS AND THERASAUNA
Toll free: (888) 729-7727
Web site: www.therasauna.com
E-mail: qcaspas@qcaspas.com

NANOBAC LABS
Phone: (813) 264-2241
Web site: www.nanobaclabs.com

NUTRI-WEST

Toll free: (800) 451-5620

Call to order Natural Change Cream.

INTERGRATIVE THERAPEUTICS, INC.

Toll free: (800) 931-1709

Use order code PCP5266 to order Indoplex.

PREVEBTHIUM INTERNATIONAL, INC.

Toll free: (800) 755-1327

Call to order Redoxal HMF (dl-methionine).

NOTES

CHAPTER 1
THE MENACE OF MERCURY

1. "ATSDR/EPA Priority List," Agency for Toxic Substances and Disease Registry, U.S. Department of Health and Human Services, 1995.
2. Susan Schober, et al., "Blood Mercury Levels in US Children and Women of Childbearing Age, 1999–2000," *Journal of the American Medical Association* 289 (April 2, 2003): 1667–1674.

CHAPTER 2
THE DEBACLE OF DEHYDRATION

1. F. Batmanghelidj, *Your Body's Many Cries for Water* (Falls Church, VA: Global Health Solutions, Inc., 1997).
2. "Water: Life's Basic Building Block," *Natural Lifestyle* newsletter, www.naturallifestyle.com
3. Ibid.
4. Ibid.
5. Ibid.
6. Ibid.
7. Ibid.
8. Ibid.
9. Ibid.

CHAPTER 3
THE DESPERATE NEED TO DETOXIFY

1. Otto Warburg, "The Prime Cause and Prevention of Cancer," revised lecture at the meeting of the Nobel laureates on June 30, 1966. National Cancer Institute, Bethesda, MD, 1967.

CHAPTER 4
THE DISASTER OF DEADLY EMOTIONS

1. Patty Wooten, "Humor: An Antidote for Stress," www.jesthealth.com/artantistress.html
2. George Ritchie and Elizabeth Sherrill, *Return From Tomorrow* (Grand Rapids, MI: Baker Book House, 1979).
3. Ibid.
4. Stephen R. Covey, *The 7 Habits of Highly Effective People* (New York: Simon and Schuster, 1989).
5. Karol Truman, *Feelings Buried Alive Never Die* (n.p.: Olympus Distribution Corp., 1991).

CHAPTER 5
THE DEAD FOOD DILEMMA

1. Weston Price, *Nutrition and Physical Degeneration,* 6th edition (New Canaan, CT: Keats Publishing, Inc., 1998).
2. George Malkmus, *Why Christians Get Sick* (Shippensburg, PA: Destiny Image Publishers, 1995).

CHAPTER 6
THE DIETING DECEPTION

1. Sally Fallon, *Nourishing Traditions* (San Diego: Promotion Publishing, 1995).
2. Kim Severson, *The Trans Fat Solution: Cooking and Shopping to Eliminate the Deadliest Fat From Your Diet* (N.p.: Ten Speed Press, 2003). Mary G. Enig and Sally Fallon, "The Oiling of America," *NEXUS* (December 1998–January 1999).
3. Ibid.

CHAPTER 7
THE DEPLETED SOIL DISASTER

1. M. Murray, et. al., *Encyclopedia of Natural Medicine* (Rocklin, CA: Prima Publishing, 1998).

CHAPTER 8
THE RISK OF FREE RADICALS

1. J. Bland, et. al., *The Nutrition Superbook* (New Canaan, CT: Keats Publishing, 1995).

CHAPTER 10
THE PERILS OF PERSONAL CARE AND HOUSEHOLD PRODUCTS

1. David Steinman and Samuel S. Epstein, M.D., *The Safe Shopper's Bible,* (New York: Macmillan Company), 181.
2. Department of Health and Human Resources, April 22, 1991; National Institutes of Health/National Cancer Institute; Bethesda, MD 20892.
3. Ibid.
4. Ibid.
5. Ibid.
6. Steinman and Epstein, *The Safe Shopper's Bible,* 181.
7. Ibid., 241.
8. Ibid.
9. Ibid.
10. Ibid., 240.
11. Ibid., 265.
12. Ibid., 266
13. Ibid.
14. Ibid., 17.
15. Ibid., 57.

16. Ibid.
17. "Are Your Personal and Skin Care Products Safe?," source obtained from the Internet at www.healthbiz2000.com/skin_care.htm
18. Steinman and Epstein, *The Safe Shopper's Bible*, 74–76.
19. Ibid., 93–94.
20. Ibid.
21. Ibid.
22. Ibid.
23. Ibid.
24. "Coalition Calls for Open Files on Pesticide Use," source obtained from the Internet at www.pesticide.org/OPENFilesRelease.html.
25. Steinman and Epstein, *The Safe Shopper's Bible*, 109.
26. Internet source: www.epa.gov/pesticides/citizens/pest_ti.htm
27. Internet source: www.epa.gov/pesticides/citizens/insectrp.htm.
28. Ibid.

SELECTED BIBLIOGRAPHY

CHAPTER 1: THE MENACE OF MERCURY

Drasch et al. "Mercury burden of human fetal and infant tissues." *Eur J Perilatt* (1994): 153:607–610.

Duhr, E., C. Pendergrass, E. Kasarkis, J. Slevin, and B. Haley. "Hg2+ Induces GTP-Tubulin Interactions in Rat Brain Similar to Those Observed in Alzheimer's Disease." *Abstract 493* (presented at the Seventy-fifth Annual Meeting of the Federation of American Societies for Experimental Biology (FASEB), Atlanta, Georgia, 21–25 April 1991).

Gay, D. D., R. D. Cox, and J. W. Reinhardt. Letter, "Chewing releases mercury from fillings." *Lancet* 1:8123:985–986 (1979).

Hahn, L. J., R. Kloiber, R. W. Leininger, M. J. Vimy, and F. L. Lorscheider. "Dental silver fillings: a source of mercury exposure revealed by whole-body imagescan and tissue analysis," *FASEB J* 3 (1989): 2641–2646.

——. "Whole body imaging of the distribution of mercury released from dental fillings into monkey tissues," *FASEB J* 4 (1990): 3256–3260.

Huggins, Hal A., D.D.S., M.S. *It's All in Your Head*. Garden City Park, NY. Avery Publishing Group, Inc. 1993.

——. "Monographson Mercury." Colorado Springs, CO: December 1997.

——. "Proper Amalgam Removal." Colorado Springs, CO: 1993.

Hultman, P., U. Johansson, S. J. Tudey, U. Lindh, S. Eneslrom, and K. M. Pollard. "Adverse immunological effects and autoimmunity induced by dental amalgam and alloy in mice," *FASEB J* 8 (Nov 1994): 1183–1190.

Krohn, Jacqueline, M.D. *Natural Detoxification: A Practical Encyclopedia*, 2nd edition. Vancouver, BC. Hartley and Marks, Inc. 2001.

Koller, L. "Immunosuppression produced by lead, cadmium, and mercury," *Am. J. Vet. Res.* 34:11 (1973): 1457–1458.

Patterson, J. E. et al. "Mercury in human breath from dental amalgams," *Bull. Envi. Contam. Toxicel* 34 (1985): 459–468.

Racz. W. J. and J. S. Venderwater. "Perspectives on the central nervous system toxicity of methylmercury," *Can. J. Physiol & Phsrm.* 60 (1982): 1937–1045.

Richardson, M. "Assessment of mercury exposure and risks from dental amalgam." Final report, Medical Devices Bureau, Environmental Health Directorate, Health Canada.

Svare, C. W. and L. C. Peterson. "The effect of removing dental amalgams on mercury blood levels," *IADR Abstract* 896 (1984).

Vimy, M. J., D. E. Hooper, W. W. King, and F. L. Lorscheider. "Mercury from Maternal 'Silver' Tooth Fillings in Sheep and Human Breast Milk," *Biological Trace Element Research* 56 (1997): 143–152.

Vimy, M. J. and F. L. Lorscheider. "Intraoral Air Mercury Released from Dental Amalgam," *J. Dent. Res.* 64 (1985): 1069–1071.

———. "Serial measurements of Intraoral Air Mercury: Estimation of daily dose from dental amalgams," *J. Dent. Res.* 64 (1985): 1072–1075.

Vimy, M. J., Y. Takashashi, and F. L. Lorscheider. "Maternal-fatal distribution of mercury (233 Hg) released from dental amalgam fillings," *Am J Physiol* (April 1990): R939–R945.

Don Colbert, M.D., was born in Tupelo, Mississippi. He attended Oral Roberts School of Medicine in Tulsa, Oklahoma, where he received a bachelor of science degree in biology in addition to his degree in medicine. Dr. Colbert completed his internship and residency with Florida Hospital in Orlando, Florida. He is board certified in family practice and has received extensive training in nutritional medicine.

If you would like more
information about natural and divine healing,
or information about
Divine Health Nutritional Products,
you may contact Dr. Colbert at:

DR. DON COLBERT

1908 Boothe Circle
Longwood, FL 32750
Telephone: 407-331-7007 (for orders only)

Dr. Colbert's web site is
www.drcolbert.com

Disclaimer: Dr. Colbert and the staff at Divine Health Wellness Center are prohibited from addressing a patient's medical condition by phone, facsimile or e-mail. Please refer questions related to your medical condition to your own primary care physician.